'James Paul has done us a great service
of heaven as a fluffy place in the sky or h
engrained in popular culture it can be l
like. Paul cuts through the myths and offers a clear, biblical view of heaven as a dimension of reality – where God's will is done. Somewhere we can imagine for the future, yet experience in the here and now. Paul is a steady hand and winsome guide. A must for all who long for the new creation and long to see it leak into our everyday lives.'
Alastair Gordon, artist and director Morphē Arts

'James Paul's new book on the oft misunderstood, always mysterious relationship between heaven and earth, *What on Earth Is Heaven?*, is both nourishing for the soul and refreshing for the intellect. Paul's time as a hospice doctor and, more recently, a worker for Francis Schaeffer's L'Abri Fellowship both inform this accessible theological discussion that is grounded in our embodied reality. Paul clearly illustrates that heaven is not an escape hatch from earth; it is another dimension of reality – the ultimate reality – and Christ invites us to allow ourselves to become vessels "through which the power of heaven can flow to re-create the damaged world around you." Paul's text gives a brief, highly focused reading of the overarching narrative of Scripture, elucidating the work of heaven on earth. His book is a much needed corrective to reductive, dualistic, pop theology. He reminds us that, through Christ, heaven has come to earth so that we may have life, and that this life may be abundant "on earth as it is in heaven".'
Dr Mary McCampbell, Associate Professor of Humanities, Lee University, Cleveland, Tennessee

'On the face of it, James Paul might have been expected to share the view common to so many of his Western contemporaries: the material world is the totality of existence, death is a brutal end, the afterlife is a deluded pipe-dream. As a trained medical doctor, he was fully immersed in modern scientific methods and ended up as a palliative care specialist in a hospice. But this would reveal both a lack of knowledge for James and, more significantly, a lack of deep engagement with the wonder of Christ. This book is a rich treasure, probing hope for our future that is grounded on the great truths of what God has already done. But, most importantly of all, far from being an escape into fantasy, this exploration of the wonders of heaven is truly a journey into reality.'
Mark Meynell, Director (Europe and Caribbean), Langham Preaching, Langham Partnership

'This is exactly what I want in a book of theology: a humble teacher, a good writer who reads (bonus points for frequent references to Lewis and Tolkien!) and a winsome love of Scripture. When I was a kid and became a Christian, I believed that I was saved, but I didn't know what I was saved *for*. James's book,

like a companion to N. T. Wright's *Surprised by Hope*, is a rousing reminder of how good the good news is.'
Andrew Peterson, singer, songwriter, author and founder of The Rabbit Room

'As an astronomer teaching at a Christian college in the USA, I often get asked about heaven by my students. When teaching them about stars and galaxies, black holes and other exotic objects in our vast universe, the question often pops up "but where then is heaven, where does God live?" James Paul, in this important and wonderful book, tackles this question head-on by taking the reader on a whirlwind tour through the Bible. Along the way, he dismantles many common misconceptions about heaven, reframes the question and, throughout, sketches a new vision of heaven that captures the imagination and stirs up many new ideas. Turns out, this vision of heaven has less to do with "eternal bliss" and more with the big questions of life, things that my students struggle with every day: "Who am I? Why am I here? Who should I become?" – questions about identity, calling, vocation and discipleship – and, ultimately, love. I highly recommend this book to anyone interested in heaven (and who is not?) or who just wants to grow in following Jesus in everyday life.'
Arend Jan Poelarends, Associate Professor of Physics and Astronomy, Wheaton College, Illinois, USA

'A wrong view of heaven not only makes people ambivalent about getting there but also encourages the kind of dualistic thinking that has led Christians to disengage from the world around them; to withdraw from culture and the arts, from universities and academia, from the "dirty" arenas of business, finance and politics. But the Christian story isn't about us escaping into some ethereal out of the body parallel existence. It is, rather, about God bringing heaven to earth, so that the whole creation is renewed and restored. This delightful book is both a testimony of the author's own personal journey and a skilful retelling of the whole Christian metanarrative, from creation and fall to redemption and consummation. In the process, it weaves together accessible, but profound, biblical exposition with insights from Neoplatonism to Tolkien and from C. S. Lewis to Sartre and Solzhenitsyn. It will stretch your mind, warm your heart, get you looking forwards in joyful expectation and transform your priorities in the here and now.'
Peter Saunders, CEO of ICMDA (International Christian Medical and Dental Association)

'Profound, wise, insightful, inspiring. Jim (or James) Paul gives us a fresh and readable take on the great storyline of the Bible. Read this book and discover how we can start to experience the reality of heaven in the here and now. A fresh restatement of the deeply influential and compelling vision of L'Abri.
Professor John Wyatt, neonatal paediatrician and author of *Matters of Life and Death*

WHAT ON EARTH IS HEAVEN?

James Paul is director of the English branch of L'Abri Fellowship, an apologetics ministry that offers people space to ask their questions about the truth and relevance of Christian faith. He and his wife have worked there since 2004. Before that he practised as a doctor in London, specializing in hospice care for the terminally ill. Many of the questions about heaven raised in this book are ones that people have asked in these settings. He has two sons, a grumpy cat and joyfully suffers supporting Arsenal football club.

WHAT ON EARTH IS HEAVEN?

James Paul

INTER-VARSITY PRESS
36 Causton Street, London SW1P 4ST, England
Email: ivp@ivpbooks.com
Website: www.ivpbooks.com

First published 2021

British Library Cataloguing-in-Publication Data
A catalogue record for this book is available from the British Library.

ISBN: 978-1-78974-221-3
eBook ISBN: 978-1-78974-222-0

1 3 5 7 9 10 8 6 4 2

Set in Minion Pro 11/14pt
Typeset in Great Britain by CRB Associates, Potterhanworth, Lincolnshire
Printed in Great Britain by Ashford Colour Press Ltd, Gosport, Hampshire

Produced on paper from sustainable forests

Inter-Varsity Press publishes Christian books that are true to the Bible and that communicate the gospel, develop discipleship and strengthen the church for its mission in the world.

IVP originated within the Inter-Varsity Fellowship, now the Universities and Colleges Christian Fellowship, a student movement connecting Christian Unions in universities and colleges throughout Great Britain, and a member movement of the International Fellowship of Evangelical Students. Website: www.uccf.org.uk. That historic association is maintained, and all senior IVP staff and committee members subscribe to the UCCF Basis of Faith.

To Merran – thank you for your love,
your wisdom and your faith

The L'Abri communities are residential study centres that offer people the time and space to seek answers to life's many questions. The first L'Abri centre was started in Switzerland by Francis and Edith Schaeffer in 1955 and the name means 'shelter' in French. There are now ten L'Abri centres on five different continents. Those who work at L'Abri believe that Christianity is true to reality and that God is present and at work in our lives. They trust that the Bible gives true and meaningful answers not only to our personal questions but also to the many cultural issues that we face today. For more information, go to <www.labri.org>.

Contents

Acknowledgments

There are several people on this earth without whom this book would not have come to completion. The first is our Father in heaven, and I want to say a little about his involvement, not to show how 'spiritual' I am but because I hope it helps to illustrate the way of 'trusting in the power of heaven', as I call it in the last chapter of this book.

As I prepared for a five-month sabbatical in 2018, I began to pray that the Lord would show me how to use this time fruitfully. One question I put to the Lord was if I should write a book. I didn't want to assume that I was wise enough or knowledgeable enough to do so. So I prayed that our heavenly Father would give me some encouragement if I *should* write a book, and also show me what to write about. Around a month after I began to pray this prayer, I was giving a lecture on heaven to a group of students and, afterwards, one of them asked me, 'Have you written this in a book?' That had never happened to me before. A few weeks later, I gave the same lecture to a different group and, after it, one of the participants responded, 'Where can I read about this in a book?' So I took that as the Lord's encouragement and in May 2018, began to turn my hour-long lecture into this book. Along the way, the Lord has kept encouraging me. At one particular point when I was tempted to give up, a young woman from Japan, who had visited our L'Abri community several years before, sent me an email telling me how much my lecture on heaven had meant to her. She wrote: 'No pressure, but there is someone on the other side of the world who is excited about your potential book.' How could I refuse that?

Another person without whom this book would not have been written is Peter Wonson. I didn't know Peter very well when he bounded up to me one morning after church and said, 'I heard you are writing a book. I would love to help you edit it.' So started a two-year partnership where I sent Peter each completed chapter and he would respond with edits and suggestions. But most important to me was his joyful enthusiasm, which kept me going when I would have given up. He was just the gift from the Lord that I needed. Thank you, Peter.

The final person I couldn't have done without is my wife Merran, who had to put up with a distracted and sometimes grumpy husband for two years, but did so with incredible grace, good will and constant belief in what I was doing. Thank you too Jack and Sam for keeping life normal and fun during the writing process.

I also want to express my gratitude to Mike Hammerton of MikeHammertonDesign for designing and producing the original graphics on which the illustrations in the book are based. Thank you to Philip Sampson for your help on the meaning of creation and animals in the new creation, and to Sue Halliday for your good advice on finding a publisher. Thank you to all the L'Abri workers from whom I have learned so much, and for my present colleagues at Greatham, who had to put up with a sometimes tired and pre-occupied team leader.

I want to thank the team at IVP for believing in my book and especially Caleb Woodbridge, IVP's Publishing Director, for his skill and knowledge as an editor. My prayer when I put it into his hands was that it would 'become a better book', and I truly believe that prayer has been answered.

Last, I want to thank you, the reader, for giving your time and energy to read what I have written. My ongoing prayer is that this book will help you to journey 'farther in and farther up' into the wonderful reality that is the kingdom of heaven on earth.

Introduction: Deeper into reality

'Come farther up! Come farther in!'
(Jewel the Unicorn in C. S. Lewis, *The Last Battle*[1])

I was a Christian. I was going to heaven. The only problem was, I didn't want to go there . . .

This sudden realization came to me as I was waiting to take off on a flight from London to Warsaw. I don't like flying. Because I'm a control freak, flying makes me nervous. I would be fine if I was flying the plane, but trusting my life to someone else I don't know is another matter. So I was sitting there imagining the plane crashing, contemplating death and what comes after death, when I suddenly realized that I didn't really want to go to heaven.

I loved this life. I loved the feeling of sun on my face, the taste of olives on my tongue, the comfort of a hug, the smell of freshly washed linen. I loved walking in the English countryside, I loved the colours of spring, I loved jumping into a swimming pool on a hot day and feeling the cool water make my skin tingle.

Nothing about heaven or the images of heaven I had been given excited me. Being a disembodied spirit living for ever in an amorphous, shapeless future just didn't have any appeal. Floating on clouds, singing praise and worship choruses for eternity just didn't attract me. This all felt so wrong. Surely, as the greatest joy and fulfilment of the Christian life, I should want to go to heaven.

I had become a Christian a few days after my seventeenth birthday. Before that I was an agnostic. Although I believed there must be something more to life, I didn't know what that 'more' was, or even

1 C. S. Lewis, *The Last Battle* (London: Puffin Books, 1964 [Bodley Head, 1956]), p. 155.

if it really existed. I hoped there was more than the final end of history as the sun implodes and our solar system ceases to exist in 7 billion years' time. I hoped that there was some larger story to this thing we call life, and perhaps more pressingly to this person that I call 'me'.

This desire for meaning eventually led me to re-examine the words of Jesus Christ and the claims of the Christian faith. As I thought through the evidence, and as Christian friends patiently answered my many questions, I began to discover there were solid reasons why I could trust that there was more to life than just these three score and ten years. As I began to think through the evidence for, and implications of, the death and resurrection of Jesus, I came to realize that death was not the end. Death was not the great negation of all that exists, but a future awaited those who would trust in Jesus Christ; a future called heaven. But what was heaven going to be like, and why did it seem so unappealing?

Pink fluffy clouds and fat babies with wings

Of course, the idea of heaven wasn't a total blank to me before I became a Christian. My father loves architecture and history, so our summer holidays in Europe were filled with visits to medieval cathedrals. As a child I was more interested in the cheap football shirts for sale in the market stalls that filled the cathedral piazzas, but I would dutifully enter these dark cavernous spaces and look around. I remember gazing up at the depictions of heaven that often covered the inside of the domes of these huge buildings. The paintings were often done in perspective, so that the space within the dome seemed to recede ever higher towards a sphere that existed above this earthly realm. Beyond a layer of clouds was a world filled with angelic beings, depicted as what I can only describe as fat babies with wings,[2] who were singing God's praises while playing harps.

2 These are often referred to as 'cherubs', a word derived from the biblical 'cherubim', which describes a type of angelic being (see, for example, Genesis 3:24 or Exodus 25:18–22). In the Bible, cherubim are very different from the rotund babies of Baroque art. The technical art history name for these cherubs is 'putti'.

Further above was the heavenly throne itself, from where God, a venerable old man with a flowing white beard, surveyed the earth below.

I had also picked up my images of heaven from more popular sources. I'm a big fan of animated films and one of my favourite characters is Scrat from the *Ice Age* movies. Scrat is a sabre-toothed prehistoric squirrel who has an obsession with his favourite food, acorns. In one scene,[3] following a desperate attempt to reach an acorn perched on a cliff edge, Scrat suffers a fatal fall and dies. When he wakes up, he is standing before a pair of golden gates with a central nut emblem. The gates open and Scrat is admitted to nut heaven, a land of pink fluffy clouds full of acorns. In this paradise, Scrat dances from cloud to cloud as his deepest longings are finally fulfilled. He is just about to reach out and take hold of the largest, most delicious acorn he has ever seen when a mysterious force tugs him away back to earth. His friend, the giant sloth Sid, has performed mouth-to-mouth on his dead body and Scrat has been forced to return, acorn-free, to his earthly life.

These images had informed my pre-Christian imagination concerning heaven, and they continued to do so even when I became a Christian. Whenever I thought of heaven, all I could see was fluffy clouds and rosy-cheeked babies, and much of what I encountered after becoming a Christian didn't help. Most contemporary Christian art I came across depicted heaven using abstract mixes of colour and shape, with little or no substance to what life there would actually be like. In church I was told that Christianity answered the question of how to get to heaven and that we should share our faith to save souls for heaven, but I heard virtually nothing about what life was going to be like once we got there. And I couldn't see any relevance of heaven for our lives here and now, other than as a reward for believing the right things about Jesus. Heaven just didn't seem like it would be much fun. Yet if heaven is our eternal destiny, surely I should want to be there? I felt there must be something wrong with me. As I began to think more about these questions I discovered that

3 Blue Sky Studios (20th Century Fox Animation), *Ice Age: The meltdown* (Dir. Carlos Saldanha, 2006).

there was a second problem to my belief in heaven. Where exactly was it?

At the time I was sitting on that flight to Warsaw, I was a medical student. For the previous five years I had learnt to apply the methods of science to the study of the human body. I had seen how scientific enquiry had brought about huge advances in the diagnosis and treatment of human diseases, improving the quality and length of our lives. I could not ignore the power of the scientific way of seeing the world. Yet this world view had no place for heaven. It described a world of atoms and molecules and physical processes, but there was no room for anything beyond the material universe. If heaven was real, where was it and why couldn't science find it? How could I both take the methods and discoveries of science seriously and still believe that a place called heaven really exists?

These were the thoughts that were running through my head as I waited to take off on that flight to Warsaw. Perhaps you are in the same position as I was on that plane. Perhaps you believe in Jesus and in God, but you just don't find the idea of floating on clouds and singing hymns for eternity an attractive vision of the future. Perhaps you are wondering what heaven has to do with your life here and now on earth. Perhaps you are more sceptical about faith and question how it is possible to believe in a place called heaven when science has described the entire universe, from the smallest atom to the largest solar system. If you are that kind of person, then this book is for you.

First steps towards reality

The Christian art historian Hans Rookmaaker said that 'to be a Christian means to go into reality',[4] and that was just what I wanted to do as I sat on the plane to Warsaw. I wanted to move deeper into reality. I wanted to better understand heaven, so I did the only thing I could think of, I prayed: 'Lord God, help me to understand heaven.

4 Hans Rookmaaker, 'What is Reality?' in *The Complete Works of Hans Rookmaaker*, ed. Marleen Hengelaar-Rookmaaker (Carlisle: Piquant, 2003), vol. 6, p. 213. An audio version of the lecture can be found on the L'Abri Ideas Library.

Help me to long for heaven.' I only had to wait a few months before God began to answer that prayer.

I was driving up to London from Cornwall with a friend, and to keep boredom away my friend read out loud C. S. Lewis's children's novel *The Last Battle*. In the book (sorry for the plot spoiler!), the central characters either die or pass through a 'magic' door in a stable and find themselves in 'heaven'. What I heard surprised me so much that when I arrived home, I got out my battered childhood copy of the book and reread the last few chapters. It was Lewis's description of the 'feeling' of heaven that first caught my imagination; 'The term is over: the holidays have begun.'[5] That was something I could really relate to. I knew that feeling of joy and hope and release when, on the last day of a school year, the final bell rings and the humdrum of classroom routine is over, and the endless freedom of the summer holidays lies ahead. That was a feeling I recognized and longed for. If heaven was like that, then I wanted to be there.

Yet it wasn't just that feeling which excited me. It was also Lewis's description of heaven itself. The heaven in Narnia wasn't an ethereal spirit world of angel wings, cherubs, harps and clouds. Neither was it the amorphous colour palette of the contemporary Christian art I had seen. The heaven that the children and talking animals of Narnia reached had a physicality to it. It was full of trees and fields and streams and rivers and waterfalls and sunshine. It was a world in which the characters were still themselves and still had bodies that could run and jump and laugh and eat and hug. It was a reality that contained everything of the old Narnia they loved and valued, only now those things and those people were different. They weren't less real but more real. They were 'as different as a real thing is from a shadow or as waking life is from a dream'.[6] It was a place that got bigger, and more real, and more glorious, the farther you went into it. 'Come farther up! Come farther in!' cried the creatures of that world.

What I began to see from Lewis was that I had got things the wrong way around. I had been taught to see this world as the real

5 Lewis, *The Last Battle*, p. 155.
6 Lewis, *The Last Battle*, p. 154.

thing and heaven as some spiritual shadow world. I had assumed heaven was less than the physical experience I knew and, a lot of which, I loved. However, Lewis was proposing a heaven that is a deeper, fuller, even more concrete reality than this world. Rather than heaven being the shadow version, it is this world that is the shadowy copy of the more solid and more real things to come. It is not so much that heaven will be full of things we love from this world but, rather, that we love things in this world because they are the things of heaven. This was a heaven I wanted to be in.

You may be thinking that this is all very well, but *The Last Battle* is a work of fiction, and not the Bible. But what I came to see was that Lewis was attempting to capture a biblical view of heaven in his stories of Narnia. The Bible itself also speaks of the life to come as a material future in which we will be ourselves and have physical bodies. Indeed, I came to see that the heaven the Bible describes is not a less solid place than this life, but a dimension which completes and fulfils this world.[7]

The Bible describes this future not just as 'heaven' but as a new heaven and a new earth (Revelation 21:1). The story of the Bible isn't about us escaping into heaven but, rather, about God bringing heaven to earth, so that the whole creation is renewed and restored. The purpose, then, of the Christian life is not to float off into the clouds and become a disembodied soul or an angel with wings. The purpose of the Christian life is to play our part, however small, in bringing heaven to earth.

It has been over twenty-five years since I prayed that prayer on the flight to Warsaw. During those years God has continued to show me answers to my questions and to lead me deeper into reality. Now I long to be in heaven or, should I say, I long for heaven to be fully here on earth. This book is the result of that prayer. I share with you the answers I have found, in the hope that you also may move deeper into the wonderful reality that God has created for us to enjoy. Come farther up! Come farther in!

---

7 I was first introduced to the idea of heaven as a dimension by Tom Wright in his excellent book *Surprised by Hope: Rethinking heaven, the resurrection and the mission of the church* (New York: HarperPaperbacks, 2008).

Part 1

THE DIMENSION OF HEAVEN

1
What is heaven?

Religion is the opium of the masses.
(Karl Marx[1])

When a relative of mine heard that I was writing a book on heaven, she quipped, 'Oh, you've been there, I suppose?' Her response was just quick-witted banter, but as I thought more about it I realized she had a point. I haven't been to heaven. No-one has. So how can we know what it is like? Maybe that is why it is so difficult for us to imagine heaven. After all, how can we know what it feels like to be a spirit in heaven when everything we have experienced of life so far has been in a physical body on a material earth? My ideas of heaven made it seem so 'other', so far away from what I knew of the here and now. The paintings I had seen on cathedral domes didn't help either. They made heaven so distant from the earth that the two hardly connected. I began to wonder where the idea of heaven as a place of pink fluffy clouds and babies with wings came from? I discovered that this division between a material earth and an other-worldly heaven is part of a far deeper split in reality that many of us have, whether we are religious, non-religious or even atheist. So before we explore what heaven is, it might be good to clear up some misconceptions about what it isn't.

Pie in the sky when we die?

The writers of the New Testament referred to the message of Christianity, or what today we call 'the gospel', as good news,[2] but what

1 Karl Marx, from the introduction to *A Contribution to the Critique of Hegel's Philosophy of Right* (1843).

2 The word 'gospel' is old English for 'good news' and is a translation of *evangelion*, the Greek word used in the Bible.

exactly is the good news? Many people, including some Christians, think that the goal of the Christian faith is to get to heaven. I also used to think like this. I saw heaven as a reward for living a good Christian life; as a place of 'spiritual' bliss where I could at last be free from the decay, disease and death of my earthly existence. I believed that when I died, my soul would go to be with Jesus in heaven, and that when Jesus came again, he would bring an end to the material creation and take his followers back to heaven with him. So I saw the good news of the gospel as 'Jesus offers us forgiveness so we can go to heaven', and accepted that the mission of the church was to save souls for a heavenly future. It made sense, then, that during my life here on earth, I should spend less time pursuing the temporary things of this world and concentrate my energies on the only eternally worthwhile activity – telling other people about Jesus.

That may sound to you much like biblical Christianity, but I came to see that this is actually a distortion of the real good news of Jesus Christ. As we shall explore in the rest of this book, the Bible sees both spiritual realities and the everyday material world around us as important. It does not make an opposition between heaven and earth, but tells us how the two relate to one another and, one day, will be fully combined in one glorious reality. While evangelism is very important, it's not the only thing that's important in the Christian life. The believers' hope of being with Jesus after we die is wonderful, but it's not all there is to the Christian story. When we tell people about Jesus, we are inviting them to a deeper and richer way of living here and now on earth, not just offering them an escape ticket into a better world when they die. Jesus is good news not just for the future but also for our present lives, here and now on earth. And he's good news not just for human souls but for the whole world in which we live too.

Of course, if you're not a Christian, understandably you might see all this talk of heaven as pure escapism. You may think that the hope of a future heaven makes Christians focus on 'pie in the sky when they die', rather than take action over the pressing issues that face our global community. Karl Marx, the founder of communism, claimed that 'Religion is the opium of the masses', because he believed that its promise of a life to come prevented Christians from challenging the stark realities of life here and now on earth.

If the message of the Bible really is simply about escaping to heaven when we die, then Marx might have a point. Yet, that is not the story the Bible tells. Nowhere in the Bible does it say that heaven is an escape route through which we flee from the imperfections of our earthly lives. Rather, the Bible tells the story of a God who never gives up on his earthly creation. As we shall see, God's plan at the end of time is not to destroy the world he has made but to redeem it, and rather than people escaping the earth for heaven, the Bible talks about the kingdom of heaven coming to earth. This means that Christians should not just be waiting to go to heaven when they die, but have a calling here and now to be fully engaged in the challenges that face us in this life, such as climate change, poverty and injustice. Whether you are a Christian or not, your view of what awaits you beyond this life will have a profound effect on the way you live your life on earth.

If you are a Christian, knowing what the Bible really says about the future is crucial to understanding what it means to follow Jesus in this life. But even if you are an atheist, questions of the future are still vitally important. Karl Marx may have thought that the hope of an afterlife encouraged indifference to the problems of this world, but equally one could argue that Marx's belief that death is the end of our existence led indirectly to the murder of millions of people as socialist states attempted to realize his utopian dreams of a communistic 'heaven' on earth. So if you are not a Christian, I encourage you to get a clear picture of the real story the Bible tells about heaven and earth before you decide whether or not you believe the Christian faith to be true. Many of the things we think we know about heaven are half-baked versions of the truth, influenced more by ancient philosophies, the medieval imagination and pop culture than by what the Bible actually says.

How, then, did the Christian story of heaven and earth come to be so misunderstood?

A split in reality

When I look back on that aeroplane journey to Warsaw, I realize now my understanding of heaven and earth was distorted by a dualistic view of reality. 'Dualism' is the term used to describe the division of reality into two separate parts. Like many people, I had assumed that there was a dualism between the 'spiritual' world and the 'material' one. I saw spirit and matter as opposites that were in conflict with one another. That split deeply influenced the whole way I saw heaven and earth.

Dualistic thinking goes right back in history to ancient times and appears in cultures and religions across the world. Although the details vary considerably, the common ground is a fundamental opposition between a higher spiritual realm and a lower material one. The 'spiritual' realm is primary, a place of absolute perfection and goodness, whereas the material world is a fallen realm, filled with evil, suffering, disease and death. The quest of the 'spiritual' life is to escape the troubles of this earthly world for the spiritual bliss of the higher realms.

In this dualistic world view, our lives on earth are part of that battle between spirit and matter; they are a test or a refining process, in which we must learn to resist the temptations of the material world and seek the pure inner life of the soul. If we achieve such a spiritual state, then at death we will be liberated from the confines of earthly matter to live for ever in the perfection of the heavenly realms. If we have not learned the lessons of this life, we are either punished or sent back to earth to re-enter the cycle of birth and death. In this world view, the key question that religion answers is, 'How can I escape this tainted world for the spiritual joys of paradise?' The dualistic world view is very different from the picture of reality found in the Bible. Yet the sad truth is that just as it had in my case, it has found its way into the faith of many Christians throughout the history of the church.

If you read the letters of the New Testament, you can see that the apostles already had to counter the dualistic teachings of

Gnostic religious sects,[3] which had begun to influence the earliest Christian congregations. For example, the apostle Paul wrote to the Christians in Colossae that they should resist those who teach that subduing our material nature through the 'harsh treatment of the body' was a necessary step to spiritual enlightenment (Colossians 2:20–23). But it was in the third and fourth centuries after the death of Jesus that dualistic beliefs began to have a more pervasive influence on some parts of the early church. A group of Greek philosophers known as the Neoplatonists ('neo' means 'new') took the basic ideas of Plato, the great 'father of Philosophy' (*c*.427–347 BC) and gave them a new religious twist. Plato had divided reality into a dualism between a higher world of perfect Ideas[4] and a lower world of earthly phenomena. He taught that the role of the philosopher was to contemplate the eternal Forms of things like beauty or justice, rather than focus on their appearance in the everyday things of our earthly lives.[5] The Neoplatonists were concerned that the fast-growing popularity of Christianity was weakening Greek culture, so they responded by turning Plato's philosophical dualism into a religious system that could challenge the new Christian faith. They taught that Plato's perfect Forms existed within the mind of a supreme being called 'the One', who was pure spirit and Intellect. The material world emanated from this divine Mind, but was far away from it and characterized by limitation, darkness and evil. Human beings were a dualism of immortal soul and material body. By following the right spiritual path, the soul could ascend to become part of the 'One', but only if bodily materiality was left behind.

As Neoplatonic philosophers began to engage with the early Christian church, some proposed a synergism between the two

3 The term 'Gnostic' is derived from the Greek word for knowledge (*gnōsis*), as these religious groups often taught that a specific, and often closely guarded, religious knowledge was necessary as the path to spiritual enlightenment. To read more on Gnosticism, see <https://iep.utm.edu/gnostic>.

4 These are sometimes also referred to as Forms or archetypes.

5 Of course, there is far more to Plato's philosophy than this. For a succinct and clear introduction, I recommend R. Tarnas, *The Passion of the Western Mind* (London: Pimlico, 1991), pp. 6–12. For a fun way of engaging with Plato's ideas through comic book, see Robert Cavalier, *Plato for Beginners* (Danbury, CT: Writers and Readers Publishing, 1996).

beliefs, saying that the Divine 'One' of Neoplatonism was identical to the heavenly Father of Christianity. And when Neoplatonists became Christians, their dualistic beliefs proved hard to leave behind, so they became a lens through which they interpreted the Christian Scriptures. A dualism between spirit and matter began subtly to infiltrate some parts of the early church so that Christian faith came increasingly to be seen as a battle between the lustful appetites of the material body and the spiritual delights of the divine soul, with the created earth merely a backdrop to the spiritual ascent of the soul to a higher heavenly realm.[6]

Dualism comes to church

Why is what we think about spirit and matter so important? What is the relevance of all this history and philosophy to you and me? Many of us, whether we realize it or not, are influenced by dualistic ideas that profoundly affect the way we see the meaning of our lives here on earth. Strangely enough, even atheists can have a technological version of this dualism, hoping that one day the non-material consciousness of their mind can be downloaded on to a computer so that they can live on even when the physical 'hardware' of their body has failed. When I began to think more about my images of heaven, I realized that I saw the Christian life in terms of a dualistic struggle between the material and the spiritual realms. Despite going to what I still consider to be a fairly good church, I had somehow absorbed the belief that the Christian faith was to do with the heavenly life to come and not to do with the everyday things of this earthly world. Indeed, some version of this dualism between 'good' spirit and 'evil' matter is probably alive and kicking right now in a church near you, affecting not just the way you think about the future but also the way you live your life here and now on earth. Let me give you some examples.

6 For an informative discussion of the Neoplatonic influence on early Christianity, see Tarnas, pp 106–143, especially pp. 130–137 on 'Dualistic Christianity'. Although I don't agree with Tarnas's conclusions in the last chapter of his book, his historical survey of Western thought is one of the best I have come across.

Young people often comment that the church has an unduly negative view of sex. Sometimes that is merely a desire for Christians to 'go with the flow' and endorse the sexually promiscuous lifestyle of modernity, but there is also a lot of truth behind such an accusation. For long periods of history, the church has seen sex as a 'necessary evil', as something we have to do to continue the human race, but not something that we should actually enjoy. For example, an early church leader, Ambrose (AD 340–397), taught that sexual intercourse was irreconcilable with the harmony of the garden of Eden and Adam and Eve only 'descended' to having sex after they had fallen from this state of perfection. Although this was later rejected by the hugely influential theologian Augustine (AD 354–430),[7] he continued to teach that original sin was transmitted through sexual intercourse. This theme still finds its way into today's popular culture, such as in Philip Pullman's *His Dark Materials Trilogy*.[8]

Where do these ideas come from? Certainly not from the Bible, which sees sex as a gift from God and part of the goodness of his physical creation. Rather, they come from the dualistic world view of spirit versus matter; because sex has to do with the physical body, it can only lead us away from the life of faith and into sin. It can have nothing to do with a Christian's spiritual life because the spiritual life concerns 'things above', not earthly things. A good Christian should, according to this viewpoint, ignore fleshly desires and instead concentrate on spiritual things like prayer, Bible study and evangelism. That is part of the reason why some Christian traditions teach the highest spiritual life is a celibate one, with no sex in it at all. Although the New Testament does teach that a life of celibacy is a valid calling for Christians (see 1 Corinthians 7), so they can give their undivided attention to serving Christ, it nowhere teaches that sex is sinful or the celibate life is more spiritual than marriage.

---

7 To read a balanced account of Augustine's views on sex, see W. Jay Wood, 'What would Augustine say? On sex: God's blessing or humanity's curse?',(available online at: <https://christianhistoryinstitute.org/magazine/article/what-would-augustine-say>, or James K. A. Smith, *On the Road with Saint Augustine* (Grand Rapids, MI: Brazos Press, 2019), pp. 92–105.

8 Philip Pullman, *His Dark Materials Trilogy* (London: Scholastic Books, 1995–2000).

Another way this dualism between spirit and matter shows itself is in the tendency for Christians to divide life into 'spiritual' and 'secular' parts. Spiritual things are those that relate to God, to the supernatural world or to church: activities such as prayer, reading the Bible, worship services, the sacraments, the gifts of the Spirit and evangelism. Everything else is defined as secular: our jobs, relationships, creativity, family life, education, finance, sport, recreation and music (unless, of course, it is worship music!). To grow in our faith, we must engage less with the worldly things of this life and spend more of our time and energy on spiritual things. Each church has its own particular list of what these are: for some it is having a devotional time each morning; for others a sound knowledge of Christian doctrine; for some, taking part in worship services; for others, manifesting charismatic gifts. Whichever it is, the spiritual path is one that disengages from the 'temporary' things of this world and focuses on the heavenly things of the life to come. Bible texts, such as 'Set your minds on things above, not on earthly things' (Colossians 3:2), are often used to support this point of view.

Such dualism between matter and spirit also affects the way that some churches interpret what will happen in the future, or 'end times', when Jesus comes again to earth. Verses such as those in 2 Peter, which say 'The present heavens and earth are reserved for fire' (2 Peter 3:7) and 'The heavens will disappear with a roar; the elements will be destroyed by fire, and the earth and everything in it will be laid bare' (2 Peter 3:10), are interpreted to teach that when Jesus returns, he will destroy the entire physical creation and take the souls of the righteous to be with him in a non-material heaven. One young man who had grown up with this belief told me, 'I was taught the only things that will last are the souls of men and the word of God. Everything else will burn.' Even mainstream churches, although they focus less on 'burning up', may still teach that our final destination is to leave this world for a spiritualized heaven.

As we shall explore in the rest of the book, although such dualistic interpretations may at first sight seem to fit what the Bible is saying, they do not sit well with the Bible's overall storyline that God is working in human history to restore the world rather than destroy it.

For example, in the apostle Paul's letter to the Christians in Rome, he does not write that the earth is awaiting destruction, but 'the creation itself will be liberated from its bondage to decay and brought into the glorious freedom of the children of God' (Romans 8:21). I will come back to what the Bible says about the earth being burned up in Chapter 8.

We may think this speculation about the future is unimportant, but it has profound implications for the way we understand Christian life and mission. If the earth and everything in it is going to be destroyed, then why be concerned with any of the things of this world? Why waste one's time studying biology or economics or working in secular fields such as business, politics or engineering? Why think about recycling and preserving endangered species if, in the end, the earth is going to burn? Why engage with culture or be an artist if everything we make must be left behind? If our eternal destiny is to escape to a spiritual heaven, then what that young man was taught is correct; we should spend our lives solely on the word of God and saving souls.

Sadly, this kind of dualistic thinking has led Christians to disengage from the world around them; to withdraw from culture and the arts, from universities and academia, from the 'dirty' arenas of business, finance and politics. It has led Christians to neglect social issues in favour of 'gospel only' ministries and to view the pillage of the earth's resources as unimportant in the scheme of eternity. It has led to the loss of a distinctive Christian voice that, instead of addressing contemporary issues, merely repeats religious slogans in the hope of saving souls. It has led Christians to see their working lives as something they *have* to do to earn a living, but not something that is a part of God's calling for them, here and now on earth.

The quality of heaven

I want to go back to what my relative said when she heard that I was writing a book on heaven: 'Oh, you've been there, I suppose?' Of course, I haven't been there, but the more I thought about it, the more I realized, in a way, I have been to heaven or, rather, heaven *has come* to me.

I live and work as part of the L'Abri community in Hampshire, England. 'L'Abri' means 'the shelter' and is a Christian study centre based in an old manor house in the countryside. Visitors come and join in community life while having space and time to work through their questions about the truth and relevance of the Christian faith. I first visited L'Abri when I was a medical student. As a fairly new Christian with a whole bunch of questions, it was a huge relief to find a place that took my doubts seriously and pointed me towards true and meaningful answers. It was also a lot of fun to get to know other people who were seeking to move deeper into reality as well. I still remember the day that I left after a two-week stay, because I had the distinct sensation that I was leaving behind a piece of heaven.

At the time, I put it down to the feeling that we all get when it is the end of a holiday and we have to return to 'normal life', but over the years, I have heard many guests at L'Abri reflect the same thing; they have encountered something of heaven during their stay. As I thought more about this, I realized that we had indeed encountered heaven, because we had experienced something of the quality of heaven. I am fully aware that L'Abri is not perfect. I know that those of us who work there (including myself) frequently get things wrong. I know the people who stay with us carry scars from their past, and that community life is often difficult and painful. Yet it is also a place where people experience being listened to and treated as real human beings, and where, on the whole, people are kind to one another, encourage one another, say sorry easily and forgive quickly. It's a place where people laugh and enjoy being together, and take delight in beauty and creativity.

What I came to see is that L'Abri felt like a piece of heaven because it is a piece of heaven, a very imperfect and broken one, but nonetheless a real piece, because heaven is not a 'spiritual' realm we escape to when we die, nor is it a religious experience that we can only have in church or during a worship service. Heaven is something that can infuse earthly life. Heaven is not so much a place as a quality, a quality that can permeate the activities of everyday life, even the simplest of acts, like making someone a cup of tea.

I am sure at some point in your life you also have experienced glimpses of heaven. You might have experienced it when sitting on a clifftop, watching the sun set over a sea on fire with sparkling light. You might have experienced it when putting your feet up with a cup of tea and a good book. You might have experienced it when you grasped something that was so true about life your heart missed a beat. You might have experienced it when you failed at something or let someone down, yet you were still loved by those who knew you best. Beauty, goodness, truth, love; even though these experiences may be fleeting and incomplete, they are nonetheless a part of heaven because they are parts of the *quality* of heaven. When we experience these things, there is a bit of us that wants to say 'thank you', as if they were a gift received rather than something earned or deserved. That is because they are a gift, a gift from heaven to earth. Heaven and earth are not these two separate places in opposition to one another. Spirit and matter are not rivals. Rather, heaven is something that can fill the normal everyday things of our earthly lives. As I began to leave behind the images of pink fluffy clouds and fat babies with wings, I could explore with new eyes what the Bible has to say about this specific quality that is heaven.

Heaven is where God's will is done

Does this idea of the quality of heaven match what the Bible says? Doesn't the Bible talk about heaven as a place somewhere 'out there' where God lives? Certainly, the Bible does describe heaven as the dwelling place of God. For example, King Solomon prays to God, 'Hear from heaven, your dwelling-place' (1 Kings 8:43) and Jesus teaches his disciples to pray to 'Our Father in heaven' (Matthew 6:9). However, the Bible doesn't seem to be primarily interested in telling us where heaven is located.

Although the Bible writers often use the phrase 'the heavens' to refer to the sky, sun, moon, planets and stars (for example, in Genesis 1:1 or Psalm 8:3), they are not saying that God literally lives somewhere 'up in the clouds' or 'out there beyond the Andromeda galaxy'. The biblical creation account tells us that the sky and stars are part of God's creation (Genesis 1:6–8, 14–19), and the writers are clear that God is not limited to living at a certain location within his created world (1 Kings 8:27; Acts 17:24). In a similar way, the phrase 'heaven and earth' (such as in Genesis 14:22 or Psalm 146:6) is not used to tell us that reality is made of a physical earth and a 'spiritual' heaven but, rather, is a shorthand way of saying 'the entire created order'. When Jacob encounters a stairway leading 'up' to heaven, or Jesus, after his resurrection, ascends into the clouds, we are not to understand that heaven is located just beyond the earth's atmosphere but, rather, that these upward movements point to a larger reality that is above and beyond our earthbound lives. The biblical emphasis is not on heaven as a location in space where God lives, but as the throne room of God. For example, the prophet Micaiah saw a vision of 'the LORD sitting on his throne with all the multitudes of heaven standing on his right and on his left' (2 Chronicles 18:18), and Jesus tells his disciples not to swear by heaven, because 'it is God's throne' (Matthew 5:34).

The important thing about a throne is not its spatial location but what it represents; the power and authority to rule a kingdom. The Queen sits on an ornate throne when she opens the Parliament of the United Kingdom, because the throne represents her authority as monarch to rule the country. Heaven is God's throne because it is the place from which he rules his creation. It does not mean that he is limited to living in a particular location but, rather, that God has the power and authority to rule over everything he has made. The psalmist explicitly links these ideas when he says, 'The LORD has established his throne in heaven, and his kingdom rules over all' (Psalm 103:19). And just as a king or queen of the United Kingdom pronounces from their throne the laws that will govern their land, so God speaks his powerful word from the throne of heaven, so that his will is done throughout his creation.

The throne of heaven is the place from which God spoke his creative word, so that the entire created order came into being (Genesis 1:1). It is the place from which he spoke his ordering word that gave form and shape to the raw physical matter of the creation (Genesis 1:3, 6, 9, 11, 14, 20, 24). It was the place from which God said, 'Let us make mankind in our image' (Genesis 1:26) and the first human beings came to life. It is the place from which God gave his command to humanity to 'fill the earth and subdue it' (Genesis 1:28). It is the place from where God gave the Ten Commandments to the Israelites, saying, 'You have seen for yourselves that I have spoken to you from heaven' (Exodus 20:22). It is the place from which Jesus Christ 'sustains all things by his powerful word' (Hebrews 1:3). It is the place from which, at the end of things, we will hear 'a loud voice from the throne saying, "Look! God's dwelling-place is now among the people, and he will dwell with them. They will be his people, and God himself will be with them and be their God"' (Revelation 21:3).

If we put these ideas and images together, we see that the specific quality of heaven is it is 'where God's will is done'. Whenever we encounter things on earth that are good or true or beautiful, we are experiencing something of the quality of heaven, because we are experiencing the reality of God's heavenly rule. Heaven is not a location in space but is wherever God's will is done; where things are ordered and formed and where they flourish and have their being, just as they are intended to be in God's loving purposes for his creation. In the Lord's Prayer, Jesus underlines this connection between heaven and the doing of God's will when he teaches his disciples that they should pray, 'your kingdom come, your will be done on *earth* as it is in heaven' (Matthew 6:10). This prayer links God's kingdom, the kingdom of heaven, to the doing of his will. Heaven is not a 'spiritual' paradise we escape to, but wherever God's 'good, pleasing and perfect will' is done (Romans 12:2). That is why we can experience a piece of heaven here on earth.

It is why I encountered a piece of heaven during my stay at L'Abri and why we encounter something of heaven when we witness the sunset over the sea or drink a refreshing cup of tea or read a good book or are loved well by someone. These things are part of the will of God: beauty, goodness, truth, love. They are part of the will of God and therefore part of heaven, but they are also here on earth! If this is true, then the dualistic construction of a good spirit versus bad matter, of a good heaven versus a bad earth, can't be right, because it seems that we can experience something of heaven in the here and now of the material world.

Indeed, as earth-dwellers, creatures of flesh and bone, experiencing something of heaven requires this physical world. There is no glorious sunset without the hydrogen of the sun, without the energy of light and molecules of air, and without the cells of the human eye to see and the brain to interpret. There is no refreshing cup of tea without tea leaves and water and heat and a tongue to taste it. There is no good book without words and paper and a person to write it. There is no experience of love without an embodied person to speak kind words or give us a hug. It seems that heaven and earth are not two separate domains that can never meet, but heaven can be present right in the midst of the things of this world, even the imperfect things of everyday human life. We haven't been to heaven, but something of heaven has come to us.

So, rather than pink fluffy clouds or a place for souls when we die, it would be more accurate to think of heaven as a dimension of reality; the dimension of reality where God's will is done. That is what we are going to explore in the next chapter.

2
Where is heaven?

> I looked and looked and looked, but I didn't see God.
> (Yuri Gagarin, Russian cosmonaut[1])

A colleague told me about a song she used to sing in Sunday school called the 'Blast Off Song'. Some of the lyrics went like this:

> Somewhere in outer space, God has prepared a place,
> For those who trust him and obey . . .
> 10, 9, 8 and 7, 6 and 5 and 4, call upon the Saviour while you may,
> 3 and 2, coming through the clouds in bright array,
> The countdown's getting closer every day . . .
> Soon will the trumpet sound, and we will rise off the ground
> With Christ forever we will be.[2]

I came across a poster that commemorated the first flight into outer space by the Russian cosmonaut Yuri Gagarin in 1961. It shows a smiling Gagarin looking around as he floats amongst the stars. Below are the roofs of churches and a mosque, and the caption 'Boga Nyet!', which translates, 'There is no God!'[3] The poster was a piece of Soviet propaganda designed by an atheist state to demonstrate the final triumph of reason over religion; Gagarin had been

1 These words were supposedly spoken by Gagarin on 14 April 1961, a few days after his return from space. It is disputed whether Yuri Gagarin actually said them. More likely, they were attributed to him by Nikita Khrushchev, First Secretary of the Communist Party, to promote the atheist agenda of the Soviet Union.

2 Copyright © Dorothy G. Montgomery.

3 You can see the poster at <www.theguardian.com/books/2018/oct/05/belief-is-back-societies-worldwide-faith-religion>.

to the heavens and found no God. Since that first space flight we have been able to describe more and more of the universe in terms of its material substances, from the smallest subatomic particles, to the largest black holes of far-flung galaxies. Yet no NASA space *Voyager* mission or radio telescope has ever found the place that 'God has prepared' in outer space that my colleague sang about in her Sunday school. If heaven really exists, why can't we see it?

Science versus faith

One answer that people sometimes give is that science can't find heaven because heaven is a matter of 'faith' not reason. They say that science tells us about the material things of nature, but that faith tells us about the 'spiritual' things of the supernatural world. Attractive as this answer might be, I can't agree with it because it creates a similar split in reality to the dualism we encountered in the last chapter. It makes science and faith into separate categories that have no contact with one another; science tells us provable facts about the real world, whereas faith becomes hopeful wish-fulfilment about spiritual things for which we have no evidence. The Bible itself, however, does not ask us to divorce Christian faith from reason. The apostle Peter encourages his readers to 'be prepared to give an answer to everyone who asks you to give the reason for the hope that you have' (1 Peter 3:15), and when Paul told his fellow Jews about Jesus, he 'reasoned' with them, 'trying to persuade' them of the truth of the gospel, rather than telling them to blindly believe (Acts 17:2; 18:4). Jesus told parables to get people to engage their minds with spiritual truth and used rational arguments to make his points (Mark 3:23–27).

As a trained doctor I respect science immensely. I have seen first-hand the power that science has given us to understand the workings of the body and to treat human disease. But it is often forgotten that modern science has its origins in Christian belief. It is the biblical understanding of God as a God of order, who created an ordered world, that first led early scientists to expect to find comprehendible physical laws that govern the natural world.[4] For instance, the seventeenth-century chemist Robert Boyle, was able to discover the inverse relationship between the pressure and volume of a gas by using a philosophy of experimentation which was directly derived from his Christian conviction that 'God would not have made the universe as it is, unless he intended us to understand it'.[5]

Far from asking us to switch off our thinking, the Christian faith encourages us to engage our minds with all aspects of our lives, including 'spiritual' things and the things of our faith. I am not a Christian because I just unquestioningly believe, but because I have found that the Bible gives a description of reality that is more true, more consistent and more liveable than any other philosophy or religion that I have ever encountered. It was reasoned argument that led me to faith, and the same is true for many eminent scientists, such as Francis Collins, lead scientist on the Human Genome Project.[6] So let's engage our thinking with what the Bible says about the structure of the reality that God has created.

Visible and invisible realities

The Bible itself does not divide the universe into a dualism between material nature and non-material spirit. Many people assume that it does, because the Bible says that there are 'visible' and 'invisible' parts to reality. For example, the apostle Paul writes in his letter to the Colossians that God made all things, 'things in heaven and on

4 For a concise summary of the influence of Christianity on the rise of modern science, see James Hannam's article in *First Things* (October 2011), 'Modern Science's Christian Sources: Exploding the persistent myth that Christianity impeded the growth of science', at <www.firstthings.com/article/2011/10/modern-sciences-christian-sources>. For a more thorough discussion of the relationship of religion and science, including a rebuttal of the new atheist position that science and faith are in conflict, see Peter Harrison, *The Territories of Science and Religion* (Chicago, IL: University of Chicago Press, 2015).

5 To learn more about how Robert Boyle integrated faith and science, see this entry on Robert Boyle in the *Stanford Encyclopaedia of Philosophy* at <https://plato.stanford.edu/entries/boyle/#BoylArguForExisGod>.

6 See Francis S. Collins, *The Language of God: A scientist presents evidence for belief* (London: Pocket Books, 2007).

earth, visible and invisible' (Colossians 1:16), and in another letter that God is 'the King eternal, immortal, invisible, the only God' (1 Timothy 1:17). It might seem at first that the Bible is affirming the Neoplatonic split between matter and spirit. But if you think about it more deeply, 'visible' and 'invisible' are not just other words for 'material' and 'spiritual'. Rather, what they are telling us is that there are 'visible' parts of reality that we can see and experience as earth-dwellers and 'invisible' parts of reality that we cannot see or experience as earth-dwellers. Something that is invisible, however, is not necessarily less real and solid than the things that are visible.

You might think of it like the invisibility cloak in the Harry Potter books.[7] When Harry puts on the cloak, he doesn't become less real or less material. What he becomes is invisible to normal human sight and undetectable by normal magical means. Yet he is still there; just as material and real as the world around him. People can still bump into him and he can still affect what goes on around him in the visible world. In a similar way, the Bible does not divide reality into a material realm that we live in everyday and an invisible realm of shadows and ether that we escape to when we die. Rather, the Bible says that there are parts of reality that are visible to us as human beings, and parts of reality that are invisible to us. The invisible dimensions, however, are no less real and solid than the visible ones. In fact, as we shall see, they may be even more real than the visible ones; it's just we can't normally see them.

The distinction between a visible world and an invisible one should not be new to us, because there are plenty of phenomena in our world that are not normally visible or accessible to us but are nonetheless very real. Humans cannot normally hear the high-pitched sounds of a dog whistle, or the trills and clicks that dolphins use to communicate. Neither can we normally see ultraviolet light or X-rays. Yet all these things exist. Furthermore, they interact with our everyday observable world in important ways; exposure to

7 There are seven books in the Harry Potter series by J. K. Rowling, published by Bloomsbury Children's Books.

invisible X-rays can give us cancer. In fact, there are many things in our world that we cannot detect, but we know they exist because of their observable effects on our world.

We can observe an apple falling to earth from a tree, and even calculate the force of gravity between the two objects, but we cannot 'see' what makes the bonds of attraction between the apple and the earth. We know that the normal 'solid' matter of the universe makes up only around 5 per cent of its measurable mass, so there must be something else present, but so far we haven't been able to 'see' what this invisible 'dark matter' is.[8] Indeed, some scientists postulate that there are ten, twelve or even more different dimensions to reality, most of which we cannot 'see'. The Bible talks about this kind of world. It tells us that God is the creator of everything that exists, both in the dimensions of reality that are visible to us as earth-dwellers and in those that are invisible. The invisible things, however, are not necessarily less real than the earthly ones. They are not a spiritualized world of ether and clouds we escape into. In fact, the things we can't normally see may be even more real than the things we can normally see. How, then, can we know that these 'invisible' realities exist? We can only know about them if they intrude upon and interact with our 'visible' world in such a way that we can experience and understand them. And this is just what we find in the Bible.

Lessons in transfiguration

There are many moments in the Bible when the 'invisible' becomes 'visible'. One notable episode is in the Old Testament, when the prophet Elisha is surrounded by a large army of his enemies. His servant anxiously asks Elisha, 'What shall we do?' Elisha reassures him, 'Don't be afraid . . . Those who are with us are more than those who are with them.' You can imagine the servant thinking that Elisha had gone crazy. There were only two of them; how could there be more people on their side than the vast army of their enemies?

8 See <https://home.cern/science/physics/dark-matter> for more information on dark matter.

Then Elisha prays that God would open his servant's eyes, and his servant sees 'the hills full of horses and chariots of fire'. God enabled the servant to see an army of angels in the created dimensions of reality that were not normally visible to him, yet nonetheless just as real as this world; real enough to rescue Elisha and his servant from their visible enemies (2 Kings 6:15–23).

In the New Testament there is also an occasion when three of Jesus' disciples experience something of reality that they could not normally see. Jesus took Peter, James and John up a high mountain where they saw Jesus 'transfigured' in his glory. His face 'shone like the sun, and his clothes became as white as the light' (Matthew 17:1–13). One moment the three disciples saw the visible Jesus they knew from their everyday earthly lives; the Jesus who was dressed in coarsely woven, dull-coloured, dust-covered clothes. The next moment the invisible had been made visible and they saw Jesus revealed as the Christ, the radiant King of Glory. They saw that there was more to Jesus than just his earthly dimensions, and although this extra dimension was normally invisible to them, it was no less real than the everyday Jesus.

The transfigured Jesus wasn't less material or more ethereal than the earthly Jesus. The transfigured Jesus wasn't the Neoplatonic spiritual ideal of a soul released from the confines of matter to become 'pure spirit'; rather the reverse. The transfigured Jesus was *more* real, more solid, a stunningly more complete reality than the Jesus they lived with every day. The disciples witnessed a whole other dimension to Jesus that they had not been able to see clearly before. This dimension did not obliterate the earthly Jesus but added to and completed his earthly reality. If one of the disciples had reached out and touched the transfigured Jesus, his hand would not have gone through Jesus, but would have touched a more solid and weighty reality than the earthly world around them. When this window into another dimension was closed, the disciples saw the everyday Jesus still standing there. They walked down the mountain with him, back into 'normal' life, but from that moment on they knew that there was more to Jesus than just the visible events of his earthly life.

'Not everything that counts can be counted'[9]

Of course, when you begin to think of it, there are many things that profoundly affect our lives but are invisible to us: bravery, kindness, love, goodness, beauty, truth. All these things we hold dear as an essential part of a life well lived. We can see the effects they produce in people, but they are not themselves visible or measurable. Or take ideas: an idea cannot be measured or detected with a telescope or Geiger counter and yet ideas have a profound effect on our personal lives and on human history. Karl Marx, the father of communism, came up with an idea that changed the course of world history and indirectly led to the deaths of millions of people. When an idea spreads from one person to another, to a community, to a country, to an entire civilization, nothing that we can see passes between people, but those people, communities and civilizations are profoundly changed.

Or think about morals. Science may be able to tell us the most efficient thing to do or the most effective course of action, but it cannot tell us whether that action is right or wrong, good or evil, kind or unkind. In the COVID-19 pandemic that spread globally in 2020, scientific models could tell us how many people were likely to die if we took this course of action against that one. However, they couldn't tell us whether we should prioritize the economy over people's lives, the young over the old, or mental health over lockdown. It wasn't just that we didn't have enough scientific data but, rather, science could never tell us these things because these kinds of choices exist in a different dimension to science. They are no less real. Indeed, sometimes they may be even more important than science, because without these other dimensions we cannot be truly human. I'm not saying the scientific method is wrong but, rather, we need to recognize, just because science can't 'see' something, it doesn't mean that it isn't real and meaningful. Just because science hasn't found heaven

9 The full quote is, 'Not everything that can be counted counts, and not everything that counts can be counted.' It is attributed to William Bruce Cameron in *Informal Sociology: A casual introduction to sociological thinking* (New York: Random House, 1963).

doesn't mean that heaven doesn't exist or that to believe in heaven is irrational. But where, then, is it?

Heaven as a dimension, not a location

The reason that science can't see heaven is because it is not a location somewhere in outer space (apologies to the Blast Off Song and Yuri Gagarin!). It is not *within* the space–time dimensions that we can measure with scientific instruments. Heaven is an altogether different dimension: 'the eternal dimension of reality where God's will is done'. However, this doesn't mean that it is a non-material 'spiritual' cloudscape we escape into when we die. Just because most of heaven is not normally visible to us, it doesn't mean that it is less real and solid than the earth. Indeed, in the biblical structure of reality, the reverse is true: heaven is more solid than the earthly dimensions we live in every day. It is not a 'spiritual' dimension into which we flee to escape earthly reality, but a dimension that is coming to earth to complete and fulfil earthly reality. This is what the disciples witnessed when they saw Jesus transfigured; the earthly Jesus they knew was stunningly completed and fulfilled by the dimension of heaven. To help us understand more of what it looks like for the dimension of heaven to be added to the earth, I want to introduce you to Flatland.

Welcome to Flatland

This part of the book may feel a little like that moment in a sci-fi film when the characters begin to explain about time travel, using elastic bands and paperclips. But if you stay with me during our visit to Flatland, I think you will come away with some useful ideas and images that help you engage more deeply with God's reality.

I'm sure you are aware that as earth-dwellers, we live in four dimensions: the three dimensions of space – length, width and height – and the fourth dimension of time. But I want you to imagine the world of Flatland, in which there are only two dimensions: length and width.[10] In Flatland there is no height or depth. There is no above or below, no up or down. There is only left and right, forwards and backwards. Flatland is therefore like a sheet of paper, which has width and length but no thickness whatsoever.

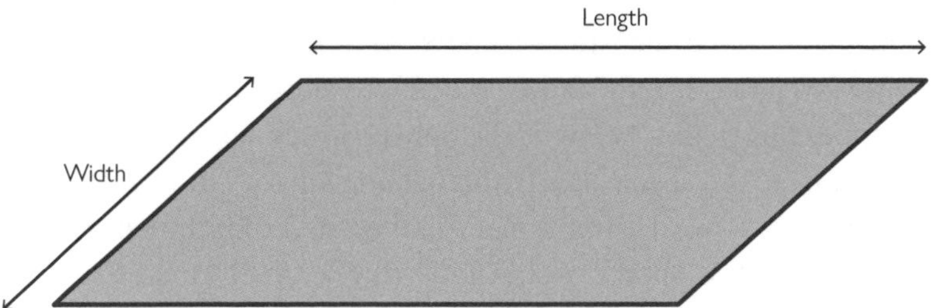

Figure 1 **The two dimensions of Flatland**

Of course, in our world a piece of paper always has some very small thickness, even if it is hardly visible – which goes to show how difficult it is for us to imagine anything outside our four-dimensional world. However, for the purposes of this thought experiment, you have to try to imagine a world where there are only two dimensions, length and width. In Flatland there are triangles and squares, polygons and circles, but no solid shapes. There are no pyramids, cubes, polyhedrons or spheres, because a solid shape would require a third dimension. The citizens of Flatland have eyes that can only see in the two-dimensional plane of Flatland, since that is all that exists to them.

Now imagine that one day a Sphere, a three-dimensional being from the three-dimensional world of Spaceland, visits Flatland and tries to convince its citizens that there is more to reality than just their two dimensions. The Sphere might first attempt to speak to the Flatlanders from above Flatland and try to explain to them what height and depth mean. However, words like 'up' and 'down', 'above' and 'below' would be nonsense to those who only know two dimensions. Furthermore, since the Sphere was above Flatland in the

10 I first came across Flatland in a short novel entitled *Flatland: A romance of many dimensions* (London: Seeley and Co., 1884), written by Edwin Abbott Abbott, a rather eccentric Victorian schoolmaster and theologian. Most of my examples from Flatland are taken from this book.

third dimension, he would be invisible to the Flatlanders and appear to them only as a disembodied voice. From this they might deduce that 'height' and 'depth' were words that described ghost-like 'spiritual' things that exist *within* Flatland but are invisible to their sight.

The Sphere might next attempt to prove the existence of the third dimension, the dimension of 'above' and 'below', by entering the world of Flatland from 'above', moving through its plane and then disappearing again 'below'. , the Sphere would appear as a circle. (You can see this if you cut a tennis ball in half; the cut surface of the ball appears as a circle in the plane of the cut.) From the perspective of Flatland, the Sphere would look like a small circle that first appears, then gets larger and larger (until the maximum diameter of the Sphere is reached), then reduces in diameter again before finally disappearing from sight. (See figure 2 opposite.) The Flatlanders might be filled with wonder at this unusual phenomenon, but they would more likely assume it to be a conjuring trick than proof of a third dimension.

The only way that the Sphere could prove the existence of the third dimension would be to change the nature of a Flatlander's eye so that it could swivel up and down. Then, at last, they would be able to see 'above' and 'below' the plane of Flatland and gaze into the third dimension. The Sphere could then carry a Flatlander up into Spaceland so that for the first time they can see it from above, from the perspective of the third dimension. Only then would the Flatlander understand that the words 'above' and 'below' are not names for shadowy things that exist *within* the dimensions of length and width, but words that describe a totally new dimension, a dimension that adds an almost infinite amount of height and depth to the world in which they live.[11] For, as figure 3 (opposite) shows, a two-dimensional plane such as Flatland can fit into the three-dimensional cube of Spaceland almost an infinite number of times.

The third dimension, then, is not a shadow world or an ethereal cloudscape when compared to Flatland. It is not *less* solid than

11 For a beautifully animated depiction of a 3D object interacting with a 2D plane as a picture of how God relates to us, watch the video 'God' from Bible Project, available online at <https://bibleproject.com/explore/god>.

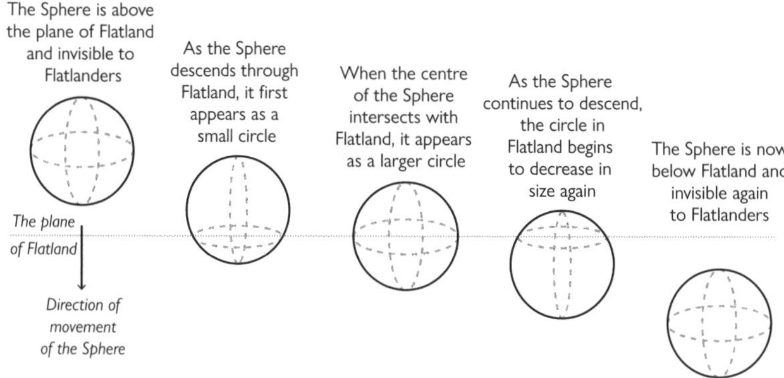

Figure 2 **A Sphere moves through Flatland**

Flatland but, rather, adds a whole new quality of solidity to Flatland, so that squares are transformed into cubes, circles into spheres, and triangles into pyramids. The third dimension adds weightiness to two-dimensional reality, and this is just what the dimension of heaven does to the earth.

What does time add to space?

To help us understand what it means for a dimension to add a whole new quality to reality, it might help us to think about the dimensions

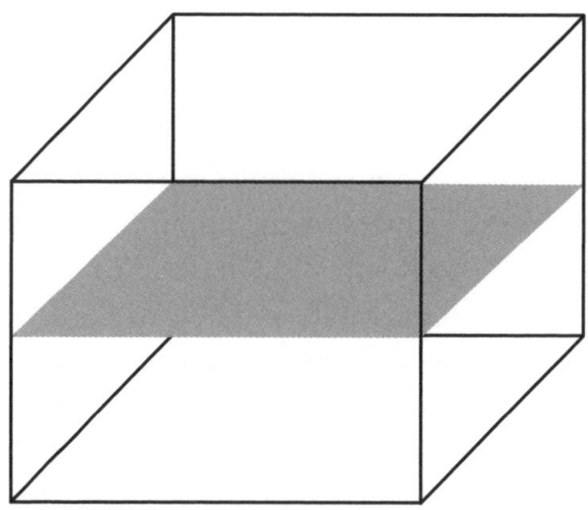

Figure 3 **The plane of Flatland surrounded by Spaceland**

in which we live, those of space and time. What happens when we add the dimension of time to the three dimensions of space? If I take this table I am sitting at while writing this book, I can describe it within the three dimensions of space. It is 92 cm long by 70 cm wide by 60 cm high. Now let's add the fourth dimension of time and see what happens. When we add the dimension of time, we don't just add more centimetres to the size of the table. We add something totally different, a totally new quality to the table. A whole new axis of reality is created. Now the same table has not only the axes of space but also the axis of time. We are not just able to measure the size of the table, but we can measure something entirely different: its history. We can now say: 'This table was made in 1896, it was repaired in 1952, it has been in our home since 2000 and it was repainted in 2018.' Time adds a whole new dimension to the table that didn't exist before. Even though time is in one sense 'invisible' to us, the dimension of time intersects and interacts significantly with the dimensions of space. Time adds to the reality of the table. It makes the table deeper and richer and more substantial than before. The physical size of the table doesn't change when we add time, but the meaning of the table increases almost infinitely.

Meaning is the connection between things. In three dimensions, the meaning of the table is limited because it is only connected to space. We can say the table is such and such a size, with four legs, it is in my dining room and it has a blue discolouration of the surface at one corner, but we can say little else. With the addition of time we can describe many more connections of that same table. We can describe how it relates to the furniture fashions of 1896 when it was made, and how my grandfather bought it in 1952 from an antiques shop on the Portobello Road. We can describe how years later it became our family dining table, and how a couple of years ago I finally got around to sanding and repainting the scuffed and scarred top. I have memories of family mealtimes, of important conversations, of dinner parties with friends, of birthday celebrations with cakes and candles; all of which have taken place at that table. In the dimension of time I know the meaning of the blue discolouration in one corner; how our 8-year-old son was painting a picture when he accidentally knocked over the blue pot of paint, which stained the wood.

The quality of time adds a vast richness of connections to reality that space on its own could never possess. At any given point in space, the table connects with an almost infinite number of points in time, so that the reality of the table expands from its simple dimensions of 92 cm by 70 cm by 60 cm into an almost inexhaustible network of people, events, places, fashions, memories and emotions. This enrichment is just what the dimension of heaven does to the earth. It does not replace the earth or overwhelm the earth. It is not a place we escape into. Rather, heaven brings a whole new quality that adds an inexhaustible depth of richness to the things of the earth; the inexhaustible richness of 'where God's will is done.' But what exactly does it look like when the dimension of heaven intersects with the dimensions of earth?

The necessity of revelation

One of the things that the story of Flatland shows us is just how difficult it is for us earth-dwellers to imagine what the dimension of heaven might bring to the earth. Like Flatlanders, we are more likely to imagine that what we can't see or what science can't detect is less real than our world. Perhaps this is why we so often revert to images of heaven as a land of pink fluffy clouds and fat babies with wings. It's just so hard for us to get our heads around what another dimension might mean. As we shall see in the following chapters, it has not always been this way. Once, the dimensions of heaven and earth were joined and human beings lived quite 'naturally' *in* heaven *on* earth. But at a certain time, those dimensions were torn apart and our knowledge of heaven dwindled until it became the stuff of fluffy clouds and disembodied spirits. If we are ever going to understand what heaven means for the earth, then we need someone, like the Sphere does to the Flatlanders, to reveal the reality of heaven to us. This is just what God has done in the Bible. The Bible is God revealing to us earth-dwellers the meaning of the dimension of heaven, the dimension of his will, for our lives here on earth.

To those of us brought up to believe that scientific truth is the only truth, the idea of revealed knowledge might seem strange, but actually it is a way of knowing that we all rely on every day. In the L'Abri community I meet new people most days of the week. When I meet someone, the first thing I do is ask their name. This is not something I can discover through science. I cannot devise an experiment that would reveal their name to me. Neither is it something I could deduce by reasoning or intuit by imagination. I must ask them, and they must reveal their name to me. The same is true for their entire life story. Science, or reason or imagination, cannot tell me where they were born or how many siblings they have, or what their parents do, or where they went to school, or what traumas they have suffered and what questions they have. Such knowledge can only come by 'revelation', by them revealing it to me.

Of course, they may tell me something that is false, so I have to weigh up whether they are a reliable truth-teller. I will also use reason as I listen to their story to see that it makes sense and rings true to the world I know. I may even use my imagination to help me enter more deeply into the experiences they tell me about, but just because this kind of knowledge isn't discernible by science, it doesn't mean that it isn't true or real. When we stop to think about it, a lot of what we 'know' from science is also revealed to us. Robert Boyle developed his scientific methodology because it was revealed to him in the Scriptures that the world would be ordered by a God of order rather than by him deriving this knowledge from science itself. We have not done the scientific experiments ourselves or worked out all the steps of causation from first principles but, rather, most of the scientific knowledge we possess has been revealed to us by our teachers and professors. Good teachers help us understand things that we could not grasp without their help. In order to learn, we therefore have to trust the teacher's authority to describe this knowledge, and when we do so, we gain a new and exciting vision of our universe.

The man from heaven

The Bible is revealed knowledge. It is a record of a loving God revealing the dimension of heaven to human beings; human beings who have lost all true sense of heaven and become mere earth-dwellers. God wants to reveal to us that we were not meant to live only within the dimensions of the earth but were created to live as part of a far bigger reality. He wants to show us why it is that heaven and earth are now separated. Most of all he wants to reveal to us what he is doing in human history to bring them together again. The Bible is revelation that we can trust because it comes from someone who has the knowledge and authority to describe earth and heaven, because he is the author of both. It is revelation that we can trust because at its very centre is not a God who stands at a distance but a God who steps *into* human history, who becomes an earth-dweller himself and in time and space performs the final act that will reunite the dimensions of heaven and earth.

It is this deeper, fuller reality that the three disciples witnessed when Jesus was transfigured on the mountain. They realized that here was not just a wise man or another prophet, but a 'heavenly man' (1 Corinthians 15:47–49). At the transfiguration, their eyes were opened to see that here was someone who was not just a part of the visible world, but also part of the dimension of heaven, and that he had come not merely to show them heaven, or take them to heaven, but to bring heaven to earth.

It is this story of heaven and earth united, divided and brought back together by Jesus Christ that we will explore in the next few chapters.

Part 2
THE STORY OF HEAVEN AND EARTH

3
Dimensions united

The world is charged with the grandeur of God.
It will flame out, like shining from shook foil;
It gathers to a greatness, like the ooze of oil
Crushed.
(Gerard Manley Hopkins, 'God's Grandeur', 1877)

When I was a child, my dad used to make up stories to keep me and my brothers occupied on long journeys or while waiting for food to arrive at a restaurant. I was probably only three when I decided that I too would tell a story. 'Once upon a time,' I started, 'there was a boy . . . the end.' It wasn't much of a story, but I remember my mother encouraging me that though it was brief, my tale had the three classic ingredients of all good stories: a beginning, a middle and an end.

'In the beginning . . .'

The Bible is a story with a beginning, a middle and an end. It begins, like all good stories do, 'in the beginning', with the Creator God who makes 'the heavens and the earth' (Genesis 1:1). God makes the entire material universe: the sun, the moon, the stars and the planets; the sky, the land, the sea, the plants, fishes, birds and land animals; and last of all he creates humankind. God gives human beings a special status that is unlike any other of his creations, that of being 'made in his own image, in the image of God' (Genesis 1:27). The Near Eastern world in which the Bible was written was full of images. Every nation had its idols, its statues of the gods, which represented the presence of those gods on earth. But the Hebrew people of the Old Testament were banned from making images of

God (Exodus 20:4) because God himself had already made his image on earth: humanity. Just as a statue was supposed to represent the power and authority of a god to rule earth, so the one true God had chosen humankind to be his representative on earth. We were to carry out his will for this planet, to be stewards of his creation.

A steward is someone who looks after a house or an estate on behalf of an owner. The steward is given authority by the owner to manage all the day-to-day running of the estate, but they do so according to the owner's will and plan. They can use their own creativity in carrying out their tasks, but the overall plan must be in accordance with their master's wishes. In the same way, humans are the beings whom God has chosen to be stewards of the earth, to carry out his plans and purposes for the earth. We are therefore beings who were created to live *on* earth but *in* the dimension of heaven. For if heaven is the dimension where God's will is done, and if humans were created to do God's will on earth, then humans were created to live on earth in heaven. This leaves a question: what is God's will for the earth?

For many years after becoming a Christian I was taught that God from the beginning had made the whole world a completely perfect place. This gave me the impression that humans were created merely to hang around and make sure they didn't spoil this perfection. Then, one day, I began to see that the Bible says something quite different. The second chapter of the book of Genesis tells us that after God had created the first human, God 'planted a garden in the east, in Eden; and there he put the man' (Genesis 2:8). This garden was a perfect place, containing all that the man needed to live and to flourish. We tend to assume that the whole earth was perfect and complete, just like this garden. However, the Bible describes Eden as having a very particular geographical location. Eden is not just a metaphor for the whole earth. The writer tells us: 'A river watering the garden flowed from Eden; from there it was separated into four headwaters,' the 'Pishon', 'Gihon', 'Tigris' and 'Euphrates' (Genesis 2:10–14). At least three of these rivers are identifiable today.[1] Even

1 The Tigris and Euphrates today have their sources in Turkey and flow through Iraq into the Persian Gulf. There is debate over the identity of the river Gihon, but some scholars have located it as rising from the Gihon Spring near Jerusalem.

though we can't be exactly sure where Eden was located, the thrust of what the writer is telling us is that the garden of Eden was a particular place on earth.

God placed the man in this garden 'to work it and take care of it' (Genesis 2:15) and he created the first woman to join the man in this task. This garden was the place where God was present on earth, the place from which he gave his commands, and the place where the first man and woman were to carry out God's heavenly will of caring for his earthly creation. It was where heaven and earth met, where the dimension of heaven touched the dimensions of earth; or to use the language of Flatland, where the third dimension met the two-dimensional. However, Eden wasn't the whole earth. Eden was a garden paradise, but the rest of the earth still had to be brought fully into God's purposes, fully joined with the dimension of heaven. It was for this task that God created human beings.

The Eden Project

In the UK, in the county of Cornwall, there is a place called the Eden Project.[2] Within a series of specially designed geodesic domes, visitors can explore two unique biomes from our planet earth. A biome is a distinct community of plants and animals that come from a particular physical environment. For example, a rainforest is a biome, as is the desert or the Mediterranean. When you visit the Eden Project, in one dome you can experience the climate and plants of the of the Amazon jungle, and, in another, the fantastic flora of the west coast of Australia. Inside each dome there is the perfect environment for the plant and animal life of that biome to flourish and grow together in harmony. Outside the dome those plants and animals wouldn't flourish because the environment is not right for them.

Now, it might help to imagine the garden of Eden as being like the inside of one of these domes. The garden was the perfect environment for plants, animals and human beings to live together in

2 See <www.edenproject.com>.

harmony. God gave human beings the task of working in the garden and taking care of it (Genesis 2:15) so that it would quite literally be 'heaven on earth', a place where God's good and loving will was done on earth. However, outside the garden the earth was not yet fully as God intended it to be. I am not saying that the rest of the earth was not good, or that God had somehow made a mistake in creating it. God says seven times in his creation account that what he created was 'good' (Genesis 1:4, 10, 12, 18, 21, 25, 31). The universe was 'charged with the grandeur of God', and there was not one thing wrong with what God had made. However, it wasn't yet everything God intended it to be. The earth outside Eden was good, but it wasn't yet complete.

Of course, God could have made the whole earth just like the garden, but he didn't. Instead he invited humanity to join him in the task of making what lay outside the garden as heavenly as what was inside, of extending the boundaries of Eden, bit by bit, until the whole earth was a heavenly place. Human beings were created by God to be the doorway through which heaven's rule would come to the whole earth.

A doorway for the heavenly dimension

You could think of the world outside Eden as being like the two-dimensional world of Flatland. Flatland is good, but there is a lot more to reality than just its two dimensions. There is a third dimension, which adds to Flatland the wonders of height and depth. In the same way, the earth outside Eden was good but there was a whole lot more to the earth than just the raw material from which it was made. There were the glorious heights and depths of what the earth would be when it was brought under the loving order of heaven. It was this task that God gave to humanity, and by carrying out this task they would bring the dimension of heaven, the dimension of God's will, to the whole earth.

This is the meaning of the word 'blessed'. The Genesis creation account tells us that for six days God had formed and filled his creation, but that on the seventh day he rested and 'blessed the seventh day and made it Holy' (Genesis 2:3). To bless something means to desire its increase, to make something larger, and richer and deeper and more weighty. God intended that his creation would continue to increase beyond the six days of his special work of creation. Human beings were God's chosen representatives to carry out this work of increase. God had so far done all the work, but now he was commanding human beings to continue that work. He commissioned humanity to 'Be fruitful and increase in number; fill the earth and subdue it. Rule over the fish of the sea and the birds of the air and over every living creature that moves on the ground' (Genesis 1:28). God gave the creatures he had created in his image the joy-filled task of making not just Eden but the whole earth into the heavenly place that God intended it to be. Humans were to be a doorway for the dimension of heaven to come to the whole earth.

In the biblical world view, the earth and all that it contains is not just a temporary backdrop for the more important 'spiritual' journey of the human soul to heaven. Caring for God's creation *is* the spiritual quest that God gave humanity. I use the word 'spiritual' here not in the sense of 'supernatural' or 'other-worldly' but in what I think is its proper biblical meaning of 'filled and empowered by the life-giving Spirit of God'. The spiritual life for us human earth-dwellers is not a life that has to do with far-away other-worldly things, but a life that is filled and empowered in the here and now of earthly life by the life-giving Spirit of God. The word used for 'spirit' in both Old and New Testaments has the meaning of 'exhaled breath', and is strongly associated with the idea of life. This is why Jesus 'breathes out' the Holy Spirit on his disciples (John 20:22). 'God is Spirit' (John 4:24) not because he is made from some non-material shadow substance but because he is the great Giver of Life, who breathed out his life to his creation, and who desires to share that life with all who will receive him. God's plan was not that there should be a dualism between heaven and earth, but that heaven and earth should be united in one glorious reality. Human beings were created by God to participate in his plan to bring the good and loving order of heaven to the whole world, so that not just the garden but the whole earth would become a heavenly place, a place where God's will was done. The process that God had started in the garden, human beings were to bring to completion.

Forming and filling the creation

You can see that God wanted human beings to continue the work he had started in the particular words that the author of the book of Genesis uses. We read that when God first created the raw materials of the universe, the earth was still 'formless and empty, darkness was over the surface of the deep' (Genesis 1:2). During the next six days God resolves this problem of formlessness and emptiness by giving form to his creation and by filling it. In the first three days, God gives form to the formlessness by creating boundaries between day and night, the waters above and the waters below, the land and the seas, and the various kinds of vegetation. In the following three days, he fills the emptiness of the spaces to which he has just given form. On day four, God fills day and night with the sun, moon and stars. On day five, he fills the sky with birds, and the seas with fish, and on day six he fills the land with different kinds of animals and, finally, with human beings. For these six days God has formed and filled his creation, but on the seventh day he stops this work and instead gives the ongoing work of forming and filling to human beings. This is clearly stated in God's command to humanity to 'fill' the earth and 'subdue' it (Genesis 1:28).

'Subdue' can be translated 'order' or 'give form to'. In other words, human beings are to continue God's work of forming and filling the creation. It is as if God says to humanity, 'I have taken the creation so far. Now it's your turn to continue the work of making it the glorious place I intend it to be.' The work of creation did not stop at verse 3 of the second chapter of Genesis, when God rested, but God wanted it to continue, as his chosen representatives carried on the work of bringing the order of heaven to his whole world. God had started off this work by giving humanity a heavenly garden, but his purpose was for humanity to make the whole earth just as heavenly as this garden. I don't fully understand why God chose to do it this way. He could have done it another way, but this is the dignity that God gave to the human race; he chose us to be a part of his unfolding plan to unite the dimensions of heaven and earth.

Human civilization is part of God's plan

What would Adam and Eve need in order to carry out God's plan to make the whole earth heavenly? One thing they would need is time; it would take time and history to make the whole earth as God intended it to be. And they would also need more people. That is why God commanded Adam and Eve to 'Be fruitful and increase in number' (Genesis 1:28). It would take more than just two people to bring the whole earth under God's good and loving will. So they would need committed male–female sexual relationships and they would need sex, and they would need childrearing and families and they would need to develop words and systems of education to teach each generation how to care for God's world. They would also need to use their minds to understand the world around them and to use their imagination and creativity to see new possibilities and new ways of doing things. They would need to develop theories of how things work and to test those theories and learn how to quantify and to measure. They would need to develop tools to help them in their work.

For example, outside the garden there might be a desert in which it was too dry for plants to grow, so Adam and Eve and their descendants would have to learn how to dig irrigation ditches to take water to make that land fertile, and invent spades that would help them in this task. As they gained more knowledge and practised more creativity, they would be able to develop more complex tools and technologies to assist them in their tasks. They would learn about agriculture and biosystems, about animal husbandry and veterinary science. They would need buildings to live in and to shelter them from the elements, so they would need to develop skills in architecture, construction and civil engineering. As human communities became larger, they would need ways of organizing and governing those communities, and they would need laws to demarcate boundaries. They would need to travel and trade between communities, so they would need to know how to build roads and bridges, wheels and vehicles. They would also need art, music, literature and theatre as creative ways to understand the world in which they lived and to bless one another with that knowledge.

I am sure there are many areas of human life that I have left out, but I hope you get the idea. In order to carry out God's plan of making the whole earth heavenly, human beings would need to develop all the facets of what we call 'human civilization'. Human history and civilization are not just accidents of being human, or something that developed after God's plan went wrong. Human civilization is part of God's plan for his creation. His plan for his creation wasn't that once it was created it would remain the same for ever and ever. His plan was for creation to be a dynamic, ever increasing, ever unfolding story as humanity brought to fullness the infinite goodness of the ways in which heaven could be brought to earth. If you like, Eden was a colony of heaven on earth and from there heaven was to spread out in all directions and in all the endless unfolding possibilities of human civilization, until the whole earth had become a heavenly place. As the theologian Al Wolters expresses it, the vast array of human civilization is 'a display of the marvellous wisdom of God in creation and the profound meaningfulness of our task in the world. We are called to participate in the ongoing creational work of God, to be God's helper in executing to the end the blueprint for his masterpiece.'[3]

A masterpiece defaced

What, then, has gone so wrong? When we look around at our world and at the history of the human race, we see 'human un-civilization' rather than 'human civilization'. We see history littered with gross acts of destruction and evil, with wars and genocide, slavery, despotic leaders, racism, the degradation of women, prejudice and injustice. We see science and technology used as a means to power rather than

3 Al Wolters, *Creation Regained: Biblical basics for a reformational worldview* (Grand Rapids, MI: Eerdmans, 2nd edn, 2005), p. 44.

to serve. We have learned to fear the weapons that our knowledge has enabled us to make because they have the potential to destroy the whole earth. We see trade and commerce that makes the rich richer and the poor work harder and harder just to survive. We see the natural resources of our planet plundered and our environment polluted. We see art used as propaganda to deceive and pornography to enslave. Everywhere we look, we see divisions and hatred and suspicion and fear.

It is not that there haven't been many good things to come from human civilization; there have been wonderful works of art and music, incredible feats of building and engineering, mutually beneficial inventions and technologies, inspiring acts of bravery and self-sacrifice. However, the sad truth is that every good faculty, every advance in knowledge, every technological development, every form of creativity, every human endeavour, has at some point been twisted and distorted from what it was meant to be in God's 'marvellous wisdom' for his creation. If God's creation was intended to be a masterpiece, then surely it is a masterpiece gone wrong. What, then, has happened to God's good plan?

The world's most dangerous predator

My wife is South African and on visits to see her family we often take our children to the Two Oceans Aquarium in Cape Town. The exhibit my children love best is a water-filled tank about the size of a large hall, which contains several reef sharks. As they glide past, with only a few centimetres of glass separating you from their razor-sharp teeth, you can almost hear them saying, 'If you were the other side of this glass, you would be my lunch!' Around the walls of the room are photographs and posters informing you about the different types of shark that swim off the coast of southern Africa, and, of course, the great white shark features prominently. However, as you leave the shark room there is a final exhibit, which says, 'Come and see the world's most dangerous predator.' I found myself thinking, 'What could be more dangerous than a great white? What deadly killer could be more fearsome?' As you walk towards the exhibit you see that it consists of just a simple mirror, and you find yourself staring at your own face.

In 2017 there were about 85 shark attacks worldwide but only 5 humans died from those attacks. During the same year over 370,000 people died as a result of direct war violence,[4] approximately 500,000 children died from preventable diarrhoeal illnesses,[5] more than 40 million human beings were enslaved[6] and over 40,000 people each day of the year were forced to flee their homes because of persecution or conflict.[7] What has gone so horribly wrong with our world? If God's plan was for humanity to be his co-workers in bringing heaven to earth, why do so many people live in what would better be described as a living hell? The Bible's explanation is that a cataclysmic event occurred in human history that has divided the dimensions of heaven and earth and redirected the whole trajectory of human civilization.

4 Figures from 'The Cost of War Project', at <https://watson.brown.edu/costsofwar>.

5 Reported by UNICEF, at <https://data.unicef.org/topic/child-health/diarrhoeal-disease>.

6 Report in *The Guardian*, 19 September 2017. See <www.theguardian.com/global-development/2017/sep/19/latest-figures-reveal-more-than-40-million-people-are-living-in-slavery>.

7 Figures from UNHCR. See <www.unhcr.org/uk/news/press/2018/6/5b27c2434/forced-isplacement- above-68m-2017-new-global-deal-refugees-critical.html>.

4
Dimensions divided

Knowledge forbidden?
Suspicious, reasonless. Why should their Lord
Envy them that? Can it be a sin to know?
Can it be death?
(John Milton, *Paradise Lost*[1])

Every religion and world view, whether theist or atheist, has to answer fundamental questions about human life: 'Why are we here?' 'Where have we come from?' 'Where are we heading?' Yet, as we look at the world around us, there is another question that presses upon us: 'What has gone wrong with the world?' Why, when we open the newspapers, are the pages filled with stories of hatred and violence? Why is the human race so prone to suspicion and division? Why is history littered with conflict and war? Why are our societies filled with corruption and greed? Why, despite the material wealth of the West, are the communities we live in fractured and anonymous? Why do so many of us feel anxious and lost? Why has the use of antidepressant drugs surged over the past decade not only in the West but also in rapidly developing countries like China?[2]

A few years ago, I attended a barbeque at a local school that followed an educational method similar to the Waldorf-Steiner schools. While munching vegan hotdogs around a campfire, I got talking to one of the teachers and, as the conversation developed, we began to talk about the philosophical foundations of the school.

1 John Milton, *Paradise Lost* (1667).
2 See 'Antidepressant use has doubled in rich nations in the past ten years', at <www.bmj.com/content/347/bmj.f7261>, and OECD, 'Health at a Glance' report (2013), available at <www.oecd.org/els/health-systems/Health-at-a-Glance-2013.pdf>.

She described how she believed that each person had an essential goodness in his or her heart, and it was the aim of the school to help each child discover this 'true self' within. I asked her: 'If we are essentially good, why have things gone so wrong with our world? She thought for a while and then gave her reply: 'Thinking and fear.' She went on to explain how society and cultures teach us to think in ways that harm the goodness within. This leads us to fear other people and respond to them with hatred. If only we could stop thinking and reach into the essential goodness that lies within each one of us, we would be transformed people and live in transformed communities.

Although there are parts of what she said I could agree with, the Bible gives a different answer to what has gone wrong with the world; an answer that I have found to be truer to my experience of the world and of myself than 'thinking and fear'. As we saw in the last chapter, the Bible starts with the goodness of creation and of being human. This is so essential to a proper view of the world that the writer of Genesis reminds us of this goodness seven times in his first chapter. There is nothing originally wrong with the material creation or with human beings. I despair when I hear preachers talk negatively about our God-given humanity, saying that we are 'nothing but worthless sinners' and giving the impression that we must escape our created humanness if we are ever to have the slightest chance of being 'spiritual'. This kind of teaching only encourages the dualistic division between spirit and matter. No, the problem with the world does not lie in the created structure itself, or in human thinking and fear. The problem goes deeper than that – to a broken relationship.

A broken relationship

All relationships have boundaries and the most fundamental boundary that any relationship can have is the boundary between trusting and not trusting. A relationship always involves trust in order for the relationship to be what it should be. When we live within relationships of trust we flourish. For example, when a married couple trust one another, they flourish together in their marriage.

However, if one or both of them break that trust, then they damage not only the relationship and the other person but also themselves. God created human beings as creatures made in his image, capable of being in a trusting person-to-person relationship with himself. He placed Adam and Eve in the garden, in the place where the dimension of heaven touched earth, and entrusted them with a mission to make the whole earth heavenly. However, the very nature of a person-to-person relationship is that trust must be chosen. Trust cannot be forced or coerced; neither can it be automatic, otherwise it is not trust. Adam and Eve were not robots pre-programmed to make certain choices. They were real thinking beings, capable of choosing and of using their reasoning and imagination to make real decisions for themselves. In order to carry out their mission of forming and filling the creation, Adam and Eve needed to choose to trust God and the goodness of his will for them and for the earth.

This trusting relationship is symbolized in the Genesis story by two trees that were found in the middle of the garden. God had planted an abundance of trees in the garden, trees which were 'pleasing to the eye and good for food' (Genesis 2:9). There was an abundance of riches at humankind's disposal, but right at the centre of the touching place of heaven on earth were two special trees. The first was the tree of life. This tree marked the reality that Adam and Eve needed to trust God as the source of life. It was a reminder to them that they were not in themselves independent, self-sufficient beings, but they were finite creatures who needed to receive life from God. The great Giver of Life was pleased through this tree to share his life with them and provide them with everything they needed. We enact this reality every day when we eat. We cannot survive without taking in food and energy from outside ourselves. If we don't eat, we quickly waste away and die. The fruit of the tree of life represents this reality and it shows that God is willing to share his life with his creation and his creatures. Adam and Eve were welcome every day to go to this tree and receive the life that God gave from its fruit. It was this life that would give them the love and energy to bring the dimension of heaven to the whole earth.

The second tree in the middle of the garden was the tree of the knowledge of good and evil. The meaning of this tree is a subject of much theological discussion, and like many things in Scripture it has multiple levels of meaning. However, at its root, it symbolizes the boundary between trusting God's view of reality and not trusting his view of reality. I recently came across a name for this kind of trust in a book on psychotherapy; it is called *epistemic trust*, and it is the kind of trust that children have in teachers or parents.[3] In general, parents or teachers know far more about the world than a child does. They have far more experience of the world and a much broader perspective. They can therefore help the child make sense of the world and of their experiences.

When children trust in the goodness of parents or teachers to help them make sense of the world, they can go with confidence to face the challenges that life brings and grow through those challenges rather than be crushed by them. I remember my wife preparing our children for their first day at school. This was something they had never experienced, but my wife as an adult had. So she explained to them, 'At first everything will be new and strange. You won't know anyone and that makes us all feel anxious. You might be afraid that you will get lost and not know where things are, but the teacher is there to help and if you don't know where you are supposed to be, then you can ask a teacher and he or she will help you. It's good to remember that everyone in your class will be feeling the same way. The feeling doesn't last for ever. In a few days you will feel much more at home, and you will have got to know some new friends too.'

Psychologists recognize that trust in someone who can help you make sense of the world is essential for healthy relationships that facilitate growth and flourishing. It is this kind of trusting relationship that the tree of the knowledge of good and evil represents. God isn't just a parent or a teacher, he is the good and loving

3 I came across this concept in Graham Music, *Nurturing Children: From trauma to growth using attachment theory, psychoanalysis and neurobiology* (Abingdon: Routledge, 2019), p. 11. He uses research from P. Fongay and E. Allison, 'The Role of Mentalizing and Epistemic Trust in the Therapeutic Relationship', *Psychotherapy* 51: 3 (2014), pp. 372–380.

author of creation. In contrast, Adam and Eve are finite creatures, with only a limited knowledge of reality. So it is right that Adam and Eve should trust God as the source of knowledge about the moral fabric of reality, about what is good and what is evil, what is right and what is wrong, what is loving and what is hateful, what is beautiful and what is ugly. This tree represents the choice that Adam and Eve have between trusting God as the loving Creator whose purposes for them and for his creation are good, or not trusting him and coming up with their own plans and purposes. It represents the choice between trusting the boundaries God has given them, or coming up with their own definitions of good and evil, right and wrong, love and hate, beauty and ugliness. It represents the choice between trusting that God has provided them with everything they need to grow and flourish or becoming suspicious that he is withholding something from them. It represents the decision to live within the creature–Creator relationship that they have been given or to reject that relationship and head out on their own as if they themselves were the authors of reality.

God wasn't out to trip up Adam and Eve by putting temptation in their way. Rather, it represents the reality of what a relationship is: every person-to-person relationship involves a choice to live within a relationship of trust, or to break that trust. God tells Adam and Eve they must not eat the fruit from this tree, not because he is mean or wants to withhold something good from them but because eating this fruit will only lead to bad things. They are finite creatures, and therefore Adam and Eve on their own, without any reference to God, are not adequate sources upon which to base reality. They are insufficient on their own to be the source of life and of blessing and goodness for the earth. They are insufficient on their own to know how to bring the dimension of heaven to the whole earth. As soon as they start following their own wills, rather than God's will, the earth is no longer brought under the loving order of heaven, but instead it comes under the arbitrary rule and limited vision of human creatures. Instead of human civilization being the unfolding display of the marvellous wisdom and goodness of God, it becomes a display of the self-centred power plays of individuals and groups.

Humanity's God-given *dominion* over the earth becomes selfish *domination* of the earth.

Form and freedom in creation

God wasn't being a despotic dictator or a control freak. God's will for how we live in his creation is broad and free, not narrow and prescriptive. In the garden of Eden there was an abundance of trees that Adam and Eve could choose to eat from. There was real freedom to choose from among these good trees, to choose which fruit to eat each day. In contrast, there was only one tree that they should not eat from, because it would lead to death (Genesis 2:17). The picture is that the good is wide and spacious and varied and involves real freedom of choice, but the evil is just the one thing: not to trust God's goodness. The mandate that God gives Adam and Eve in Genesis 1:28, to fill and order the creation, is not the mandate of a micro-manager. It is not 'Do exactly this and only this or I will be angry.' Rather, God is inviting them to be co-workers with him; to be co-creators with him, to be co-builders of heaven on earth. His is the macro-plan, but he gives humanity real freedom to sub-create within the goodness of the form that God has given them.

It is like an architect meeting with the builders and saying: 'The idea behind this building is to be a place where everyone can flourish. It is to be a place where everyone can become more and more human. This building is to be a blessing to the people who live in it and a place of life in all its fullness. That's the plan; but what the building looks like in detail I leave up to you. I want you to improvise and to use your creativity and your imagination. I want you to discover new ways of building, invent new structures and develop new materials. I want you to embellish and adorn the building with love and care and individuality so that it is a beautiful place to live. You can ask me for guidance and wisdom, and I will be with you in the carrying out of our plans. It is a partnership between me, and you.'

This is the picture that the first two chapters of the Bible give of how things were in the beginning. There was to be a creative partnership between humanity and God that would unite the dimensions of heaven and earth. But when Adam and Eve decided not to trust God, and they ate the fruit of the tree of the knowledge of good and evil, it all went horribly wrong.

Throwing off the dimension of heaven

The Bible narrative describes how one day a talking serpent meets Eve in the garden. We are not told where the serpent comes from, only that he is 'more crafty than any of the wild animals the LORD God had made' (Genesis 3:1). The serpent is not an equal and opposite force to God, or a yin to God's yang. The serpent is clearly a created being of finite power. Elsewhere in the Bible the serpent is identified with Satan, or 'the devil' as he is often called; an originally good being created by God in dimensions other than we know of on earth, who had already enacted the same rebellion against God into which he will soon tempt Adam and Eve. Most importantly in terms of the narrative, the presence of the serpent clearly underlines that evil does not start within Adam or Eve, as if there was something wrong with the way God had created them. Rather, evil comes from outside to infect the earth, for evil is not a created thing in itself, but only and always a parasite on the good.

The talking serpent meets Eve in the garden and immediately sets about undermining the epistemic trust that she has in God, sowing doubt in her mind about God's goodness. 'Did God really say, "You must not eat from any tree in the garden"?', the serpent asks (Genesis 3:1). The cunning of the serpent is obvious, for in the very question he insinuates that God is a restrictive spoilsport who wants to keep Adam and Eve from tasting any good thing. Eve responds that she can in fact eat fruit from any of the trees, and that God has only prohibited eating the fruit from the tree in the middle of garden, but she erroneously adds that God also told them not to touch it. Already the seeds of confusion that the serpent has planted are alive in her mind. Next the serpent goes for the kill and boldly contradicts God: 'You will not certainly die,' he says. 'For God knows that when you eat of it your eyes will be opened, and you will be like God, knowing good and evil' (Genesis 3:4–5).

The serpent's insinuation is God wants to limit, restrict and keep good things from them, rather than that God is protecting Adam and Eve because it is bad for them to eat this fruit. His suggestion is that God is not good but is insecure, and scheming to prevent Adam and Eve from taking what is rightfully theirs and from becoming gods like him. The serpent is tempting them to throw off the dimension of heaven and claim the earth as theirs by right. Eventually, Eve gives in to the serpent's lies. She chooses not to trust the goodness of God, but to take and eat the fruit. She gives some to Adam, who eats without question or objection. At that moment, everything changes. They cross the boundary from trust to suspicion. When the centre goes, everything around it begins to fall apart. By choosing to distrust God, they not only reject the dimension of heaven but also the life of heaven that holds the creation together. Without the dimension of heaven, the dimensions of the earth begin to disintegrate, and death begins to take effect.

The tragic effects of a lie

The first thing that happens is that, having suspected the motives of God, Adam and Eve begin to suspect each other too. It is as if Adam and Eve look at each other and say: 'If God isn't the centre, and we are the creators of reality, then whose reality comes out on top, yours or mine? If God is no longer the definition of goodness, then who gets to decide what is right and wrong? Do you decide, or do I decide? Whose plans do we follow? How can I trust that you are defining things for my good rather than for your own?'

The open, trusting transparency of their relationship, symbolized in the Genesis story by their nakedness, is overwhelmed by a sense of shame as they realize that their desires have become selfish and self-centred. The trusting co-operation between man and woman under the umbrella of God's good purposes is replaced by a power dynamic between them as they attempt to find ways to manipulate the other one into getting their own way. Without the rule of heaven, human relationships become a minefield of power games. The existentialist philosopher Jean-Paul Sartre wrote that there are only three options in terms of human relationships: sadism, masochism or indifference. Either I rule over you (sadism), you rule over me (masochism) or we become disconnected from one another (indifference).[4] Though Sartre would not have seen the cause of this state of affairs in the same way as the Bible does, he understood perfectly the relational consequences of the choice Adam and Eve made when they cast off heaven.

The consequences of their actions would not just affect them, but their children, their children's children and their grandchildren's grandchildren, for generations and generations to come, right down through the ages to you and me today. It would spread like a virus to infect the whole created order, the whole human race, the whole of human history and the whole of human civilization. The cunning of the serpent was to take a lie and use it to change the whole course of human history. Recognizing that human beings were central to God's plan to bring heaven to earth, the serpent knew that he had to misdirect the human heart if he wanted to thwart God. Once his lie had taken root in the human heart, the serpent knew that humanity would do the rest themselves. Throwing off God's rule, human beings would pursue their own selfish desires in ignorance and defiance of God. They would no longer desire to make the earth a heavenly place, but instead they would form it to suit themselves. By throwing off God's rule, humanity became purely earthly creatures, unable any longer to see or participate in the dimension of heaven. Creatures that God had made to be the three-dimensional beings of heaven on earth became the two-dimensional beings of Flatland alone. Human civilization became an arena of conflict, as tribes and nations, peoples and races fought each other for the upper hand. The philosopher Friedrich Nietzsche was right when he described the main driving force of human history as 'the will to power'.[5]

4 For a good summary of Sartre's philosophy in the area of ethics and human relationships, see Mary Warnock, *Existentialist Ethics* (London: Macmillan, 1967), pp. 18–52.

5 Nietzsche uses this concept in many of his writings, but most explicitly in his book *Beyond Good and Evil* (1886) and a collection of his essays entitled *The Will to Power*, published after his death.

Humanity turned inwards upon itself

The term the Bible uses to describe this state of affairs is sin.[6] To sin is to break the relationships that God has made us for. Sin distorts our relationship with God, with others, with ourselves and with the natural world. To sin is to disintegrate and fracture the good and true and beautiful things of God's creation and attempt to remake these things according to our own purposes and for our own goals. When we sin, we substitute true reality with false realities of our own making. Every human faculty and every experience, every desire, every plan and every invention, every thought and every imaginative possibility becomes misdirected from God's original loving intentions for his world. From this point on in human history all human action becomes tainted with the self-centred desire to shape the world to suit our own ends. Describing this effect of sin, the reformer Martin Luther used the Latin phrase, *homo incurvatus in se*: 'man turned inwards upon himself'. However, throwing off heaven was to have another dire consequence for humanity: it would bring death.

When Adam and Eve turned inwards upon themselves, they chose not to trust God as their source of life. In throwing off the dimension of heaven, they rejected their need to receive life from him and instead asserted that they could be sufficient sources of life for themselves. Yet in reality they were finite creatures who needed to receive life from God. Without his life they began to die, not straight away, but death began to work in their lives.

A colleague of mine compares this situation to cut flowers.[7] When flowers grow in a garden they are connected to a root system. It is from this they receive the water and nutrients they need to grow and to produce beautifully coloured petals. If you cut the flowers above the ground and place them in a vase in your home, they continue to look beautiful for a while. However, they soon start to dry out, the colour fades, the petals wither and decay sets in.

6 For a thorough discussion of the nature of sin, see Cornelius Plantinga, *Not the Way It's Supposed to Be: A breviary of sin* (Grand Rapids, MI: Eerdmans, 1995).

7 I am grateful to my colleague Marsh Moyle for this illustration.

Because they have been cut off from the source of life, they soon start to die.

This is just what happens to Adam and Eve; by removing themselves from relationship with God, they cut themselves off from the life that is his gift to them. Instead they try to find other sources of life from within the creation that will sustain them, at least for a while. They begin to consume the life of created things and of each other in order to give themselves life, and they become afraid to be generous and to share, lest they have nothing left for themselves. If they do give, it is often with the desire to get something back in return or to hold others in their debt.

This is another helpful way to understand sin: sin is our tendency to consume the life of others rather than to share life as a gift with them. The problem, however, is that things within the creation are not an adequate source for life. They are limited and can never fully satisfy or provide what Adam and Eve were made to enjoy – the life of heaven. Compared to the life of the Creator himself, the things of the earth are fleeting and quickly exhausted. Just like a cut flower removed from its roots, death will eventually catch up. Mortality does not simply mean that one day we will die; it also means that without the life-giving Spirit of our Creator even as we live our bodies begin to wither from age and decay and sickness. Adam and Eve's decision to cut themselves off from God brought death, but it also had consequences that went far beyond their own lives.

Human civilization redirected

When Adam and Eve decided to 'go it alone', God's creation remained good but a new direction to human civilization was introduced. Their rebellion against God could not destroy the created goodness of what God had made, but the good gifts that God had given humanity were now redirected by self-centred human beings towards their own selfish goals. Every good possibility in God's creation began to be distorted and exploited, warped and sent awry, and even the created goodness of the dimensions of the earth began to disintegrate as heaven and earth were pulled apart by humanity's rebellion against God. The Bible tells us that even the good soil became 'cursed' so that it produced inedible 'thorns and thistles' as well as the food-producing plants that Adam and Eve had sown (Genesis 3:17–19). Rather than the earth becoming more and more heavenly as human beings creatively fulfilled God's good purposes, heaven and earth were increasingly separated as humanity threw off the dimension of heaven and pursued their own self-centred purposes for the earth.

The decision of Adam and Eve not to trust God introduced a dualism into the created order, but not a dualism between spirit and matter. Rather, it introduced a split in the desires of the human heart; a split between engaging with creation out of love for God and his good purposes, or out of love for ourselves and our self-centred plans. It led to a dualism between working *with* God to bring heaven to the whole earth or working *against* God to shape the earth to suit our own self-serving desires. It caused a division between desiring to use the good gifts of God to give life and to share life with others, or wanting to consume life and take life from others. The line between these two directions did not run between things (as if some activities in human life were purely good and others purely bad) but through the middle of everything, because the split runs through the middle of the human heart. Let me give you a few examples of how this works.

Let's think about words. Words are God's good gift to humanity. We can use them to name things and to describe reality so that we understand it better. We can use words to build one another up and encourage one another. We can use words to speak truth to one another. When we use words in these ways, they bring life. But we can also use words towards a different end; we can use words to bring death. We can use them to demean other people and to have power over them. Children in the playground call other children names that hurt – 'stupid', 'smelly', 'loser' – to make themselves feel bigger and better and the other child feel smaller and weaker. We can use words to tell lies that obscure reality and deceive others to our advantage. We use words to spread false, destructive ideas, such as racism or sexism, so that others are marginalized, while our own identity is affirmed. What God gave as a gift for human flourishing, we so often turn into a curse that disintegrates and diminishes other people.

Or take creativity. Creativity is the ability to bring something new into being, something that hasn't existed in that form before. It aids us in understanding ourselves and the world around us, and is a source of great joy both for those who create and those who receive the gift of what others have created. It leads to human flourishing as we engage more and move deeper into reality. Creativity is not only expressed in the arts, but also in everyday tasks such as cooking or gardening or setting a dinner table.[8] Creativity is also a part of science and technology as we invent new theories and new tools. Creativity is God's gift to humanity to bring life, but it can also be used to consume and destroy. New technologies, like the smartphone, can as easily enslave as liberate. They can bring hate speech and pornography right into the midst of our homes. Creativity can be used to make lies seem attractive, for the ends of personal power or group domination. The Nazi party in Germany in the 1930s and 1940s was very creative in its use of architecture, art, film and the theatre of mass political rallies, to lure an entire nation towards an evil and destructive end.

These two directions, either towards or away from heaven on earth, also affect things that we might label as 'holy' or 'spiritual', such as prayer or teaching the Bible. We naturally think that prayer must be good. It's a spiritual activity, isn't it? Yet Jesus teaches that even a good thing like prayer can be used against the purposes that God created it for. Jesus tells his disciples:

> And when you pray, do not be like the hypocrites, for they love to pray standing in the synagogues and on the street corners to be seen by others. Truly I tell you, they have received their reward in full. But when you pray, go into your room, close the door and pray to your Father, who is unseen. Then your Father, who sees what is done in secret, will reward you.
> (Matthew 6:5–6)

8 See Edith Schaeffer, *Hidden Art* (Wheaton, IL: Tyndale House, 1971).

Jesus is saying that there can be a sinful use of the gift of prayer. When you use prayer as a performance to gain the admiration of others, you are taking prayer in a sinful direction. When you pray long prayers or use clever words to show everyone what an impressively holy person you are, then you aren't loving God or your neighbour; you are using prayer out of love for self. You are using it to consume the praise of others in order to give life to yourself. This is a wrong purpose for prayer, because prayer is meant to be simple communication between you and your heavenly Father, the generous Giver of Life.

Even preaching God's Word can be taken in a direction that is against the dimension of heaven. God's will is that his Word should be a blessing to others. It should bring life and truth. It should encourage, build up, comfort and, where needed, challenge and correct. Some preachers, however, use the Word of God to bring people under their control and within the force of their personality. Some teach what is clearly not true in order to further their own agenda. This is using God's Word in a sinful direction. The direction between good and evil does not run between certain things but runs through the middle of everything, even good things like prayer and Bible teaching.

A line through the human heart

The true dualism that the Bible speaks about is not a dualism between spirit and matter, or religious things and secular ones, as the Neoplatonic philosophers taught. The real dualism is between that which is directed towards the will of God and that which is away from his will; that which is towards his good and loving purposes for his creation and that which is away from them. It is the direction towards heaven on earth or away from heaven on earth. It is a dualism that runs through every human activity, because it runs through the centre of every human heart. It is the human heart turned inwards upon itself and away from the will of God that has shut the doorway between heaven and earth.

As the rest of the Bible story unfolds from Genesis 3 onwards, indeed as the rest of human history unfolds from this point, we see the expanding consequences of this decision to reject the dimension of heaven: deception (Genesis 4:9), murder (Genesis 4:8), revenge (Genesis 4:23), drunkenness (Genesis 9:21), warfare (Genesis 14:1–2), sexual abuse (Genesis 19:5), rape (Genesis 34:2), jealousy (Genesis 37:19–20), wrongful imprisonment (Genesis 39:20), slavery (Exodus 1:11) and genocide (Exodus 1:22). The consequences of Adam and Eve's rebellion distorted and twisted every aspect of human life. Yet the goodness of God's creation could never be totally obliterated. Although humanity fell far short of the glory that God gave us when he created us in his image, that glory is still there even though it is twisted and marred by the effects of sin. Human beings are, to use the words of Francis Schaeffer, 'glorious ruins', created for glory but ruined by our sin-infected hearts. Or, as C. S. Lewis puts it in *Prince Caspian*, being descended from Adam and Eve is 'Both honour enough to erect the head of the poorest beggar, and shame enough to bow the shoulders of the greatest emperor on earth.'[9]

We are still capable of incredible acts of kindness and self-sacrifice. A mother can still love her child; there is still beauty in art and wonder in creativity; there are incredible scientific discoveries and amazing technologies that improve lives. Yet the rebellion of humankind against the rule of heaven means that things that can be used to bless and enrich our lives are the very same things that can be used to curse and diminish us. The spade that helps till the field can also become the weapon with which I strike my brother; the dignity of work can become the drudgery of slavery; authority can turn into despotism; a parent's love can become clinging and self-serving; sex can become a commodity; art can become propaganda, and so on and so on. Nothing has escaped the warping effect of sin; the masterpiece that God intended for his creation is everywhere distorted, marred and defaced.

It is this response to the question, 'What is wrong with the world?' that I find far more compelling than the answer the schoolteacher gave when we chatted around the campfire. The story the Bible tells explains both the goodness and the brokenness of human history. It

9 C. S. Lewis, *Prince Caspian* (London: Puffin Books, 1962 [Geoffrey Bles, 1951]), p. 185.

explains both the dignity and the depravity that I see in human beings – and in myself. A key reason that I find the biblical description truer to the world I know is because it doesn't just tell me that the problem is 'out there' in society and culture, but that it is also *in here*, in the human heart, in my heart. We aren't just innocent victims of an evil world. The problem with the world is also a problem that lives in me. Every day we re-enact the same decision that Adam and Eve made in the garden: we turn away from God; we don't want him or his will; we think he is too narrow and restrictive; we want to be free to be the centre of things for ourselves; we want our will to be done; we want to use the good gifts he has given us for our own ends; we want an earth made in our image, not his.

It was just this conclusion that the Russian author Aleksandr Solzhenitsyn came to, following the 11 years he spent imprisoned in Soviet labour camps. As he reflected on the history and workings of a prison system that had perpetrated crimes on a massive scale, it would have been easy for him to see himself and other prisoners as victims of an evil and corrupt system, but his conclusions were not so black and white. He came to see that the line separating good from evil does not pass between nations or social classes or even between political ideologies, but passes 'right through every human heart – and through all human hearts.'[10] Solzhenitsyn's conclusion is exactly what the Bible describes: it is the human heart, turned away from God and inwards upon itself, that is the source of what is wrong with the world.

Is this how things will be for ever and ever? Has the serpent won with his plan to destroy God's good creation? Is human history a lost cause? Has God abandoned the earth to its own devices? Or can things be made right again? Can heaven and earth be brought back together?

10 Aleksandr I. Solzhenitsyn, *The Gulag Archipelago 1918–1956* (abridged edition; London: Vintage Classics, 2018), p. 312. Copyright © The Russian Social Fund, 1985.

5
Doorways between dimensions

They say Aslan is on the move; perhaps he has already landed.
(C. S. Lewis, *The Lion, the Witch and the Wardrobe*[1])

I recently visited the British Museum to see 'Living with Gods', an exhibition of religious artefacts from around the world. As I walked through the galleries, peering into glass cases containing objects such as the 40,000-year-old 'lion-man' sculpture, or a Tibetan mask used to scare away evil spirits, or a bronze sculpture of the Hindu god Shiva performing a dance of creation and destruction, the one thing that struck me was that the dominant movement of humankind has always been to reach up towards the gods. Each artefact acknowledged the universal human desire to stretch beyond this earth and make contact with the supernatural, with the realms of angels and demons. Statues, masks, rituals, dances, incantations, hallucinogenic plant extracts – all were used in this effort to touch the spiritual world. However, as I looked at the Jewish and Christian objects on display, I saw a different story.

In the last chapter, we explored the question, 'What has gone wrong with the world?' We saw that it was Adam and Eve's decision to 'go it alone' without God that divided the dimensions of heaven and earth and derailed God's plan to make the whole earth a heavenly place. The question remains: 'What can be done to put this right? What can bring heaven and earth together again?' The most common religious answer is exactly what I witnessed in the British Museum: humanity must find a way to reach god and make some offering or perform some act of service that will please him. Then he

1 C. S. Lewis, *The Lion, the Witch and the Wardrobe* (London: Geoffrey Bles, 1950).

will allow us to escape this world of suffering and enter into his heavenly paradise.

The answer that the Bible gives, however, is exactly the reverse. The Bible is not the story of us reaching up to heaven to find God, but the story of God coming down from heaven to find us. We don't open escape hatches so we can flee to an other-worldly paradise, but God graciously opens doorways between dimensions so that the power of heaven can once more flow to the earth. Indeed, God opens the first of these doorways immediately after Adam and Eve have turned their backs on him.

'Where are you?'

In the Genesis story, soon after they eat the fruit of the tree of the knowledge of good and evil, Adam and Eve hear the sound of God walking in the garden. Instead of going to meet him, they hide from him because they are ashamed of what they have done (Genesis 3:8). However, God didn't hide from them. In fact, he went looking for them and called out, 'Where are you?' (Genesis 3:9). Of course, God knew exactly where they were. He called out because he wanted them to choose to respond to him and to re-enter a trusting relationship with him.

The Bible is not a story of people who are so religious or holy that they can earn their way into God's presence. It is the story of how a gracious God comes down to earth to meet people in the midst of their mess. In many of the Bible stories God comes to people who aren't looking for him or even thinking about him. Those we consider to be 'Bible heroes' didn't start off as holy people living perfect spiritual lives; Jacob was a swindler on the run, Moses a murderer in exile and David a shepherd-boy too young to go to war. God even comes to find people like Jonah who are actively trying to ignore him or running away from him.

This has been my experience too. My most intense, profound experience of God came when I was deliberately moving away from him. Like Adam and Eve, I was planning a very nice life for myself, without his interfering presence, and then . . . *he* came to meet *me.*

It was a shock, as it usually is when we encounter the dimension of heaven, but it turned my life around and took me on a journey deeper into reality. The Bible is the story of a God who never gives up on humanity and never gives up on his plan to bring the dimension of heaven to earth. God could have decided to destroy his rebellious creatures and start again, but that is not his way. God's way is the way of love, and as the story of the Bible unfolds we see a God who graciously opens doorways so that the dimension of heaven may once again touch the dimensions of earth.

A stairway from heaven and a burning bush

There are many such doors in Scripture, and I am only going to mention a few. I am sure if you read the Bible for yourself and look for them, you will see many more. One of the first is when a descendant of Adam and Eve, called Jacob, is on the run. Jacob had swindled his twin brother Esau out of his inheritance and was so afraid of his brother's anger that he ran away from home. Alone at night in the wilderness, Jacob has a dream. He sees a stairway, 'resting on the earth, with its top reaching to heaven, and the angels of God ascending and descending on it' (Genesis 28:12). Above the stairway stands the Lord God, who speaks to Jacob. God promises this lonely, homeless man that one day he will have both descendants and a home. He promises Jacob, 'I am with you and will watch over you wherever you go, and I will bring you back to this land. I will not leave you until I have done what I have promised you' (Genesis 28:15).

Jacob's vision has inspired the popular imagination ever since. In 1971, the rock band Led Zeppelin released their song 'Stairway to Heaven', which became one of the greatest rock hits of all time. However, Jacob's vision was not actually of a stairway *to* heaven but of a stairway *from* heaven. Nowhere in the account is Jacob invited to ascend the stairway and join God at the top. This doorway is not an escape route through which Jacob can leave his squalid existence on earth. Rather, God has opened this door so that heaven might come to earth. When Jacob wakes from the dream, he realizes that God is present, here on earth, in the small patch of scrubby wilderness where he had laid down his head to sleep. In fear and trembling, Jacob comprehends the awesomeness of the truth that the place he is standing is 'none other than the house of God . . . the gate of heaven' (Genesis 28:17). It is a touching place of the dimension of heaven on earth.

Another doorway is a burning bush. We are now in the book of Exodus, several hundred years down the line from Jacob's vision of the stairway. Jacob's descendants have become a large tribe, but they are enslaved in Egypt by the Pharaoh and forced to provide labour for his grandiose building projects. Their world is just about as far away as it could be from heaven on earth. Yet the dimension of heaven is once more on the move. The Bible narrative focuses on a man called Moses, who has killed an Egyptian overseer and fled into the Sinai desert. One day Moses sees an extraordinary thing, a bush that is on fire but that doesn't burn up. In the flames of the fire he sees the angel of the Lord God and hears God call him by name. 'Moses! Moses! . . . Do not come any closer . . . Take off your sandals, for the place where you are standing is holy ground' (Exodus 3:5). Like most people who encounter a doorway between heaven and earth, Moses is terrified, but God reassures him that he has seen the misery of his people in slavery and that he has 'Come down to rescue them . . . and to bring them out of that land into a good and spacious land, a land flowing with milk and honey' (Exodus 3:8). Moses is on 'holy' ground because, like Jacob, he too is standing at a doorway between heaven and earth.

What is God doing? Why has he opened these doors between dimensions? In neither of these cases is God opening a door in order to invite Jacob or Moses or the Hebrew people to join him up in heaven. Rather, God opens these doors because he is coming down to find his lost people. He has come to call Jacob and Moses and the Hebrew nation away from their self-centred plans, which have resulted only in slavery, and to call them back to become a part of his will. God has opened these doors because he has not abandoned the earth to its fate, nor has he given up on his plan for human beings to be the creatures who bring heaven to earth. But before humanity can once again be a part of God's plan, he must first turn their rebellious human hearts back to his will. This is why God has opened these doors. One could describe the place where Jacob laid his head, and the place where the bush was on fire, as 'new Edens'. They were places where heaven was present on earth and where God was speaking his word to his creatures, inviting Jacob and Moses to become a part of his will, just as he did to Adam and Eve in the garden. God still wants human beings to be stewards of his creation and to participate in making the whole earth a heavenly place.

An antidote to chaos

A little later, God opens another doorway between dimensions on the top of a mountain. Through a series of miracles, God has freed the Israelites from their slavery in Egypt and Moses has led them on a journey across the desert towards the heavenly land that God had promised them. Guided by a pillar of cloud during the day and a pillar of fire at night, they come to the foot of Mount Sinai where God opens another touching place between heaven and earth. The narrator of Exodus tells us that 'The LORD descended to the top of Mount Sinai and called Moses up to the top of the mountain' (Exodus 19:20). There God established another new 'Eden', a place where heaven and earth met, on top of the mountain. The rest of the Israelites might have wanted to follow Moses up the mountain, hoping to enter a spiritual 'Promised Land'. However, God did not open this doorway as an escape route to heaven but, rather, as a means to bring the loving order of heaven to earth. He does this by giving Moses and the Israelites his law, and particularly the Ten Commandments.

Jordan Peterson, Professor of Psychology at Toronto University, published *12 Rules for Life: An antidote to chaos*,[2] which became a bestseller and has been influential in many young people's lives. But God got there first with his ten rules for life. The Ten Commandments

2 Jordan B. Peterson, *12 Rules for Life: An antidote to chaos* (London: Penguin, 2018).

are an antidote to the chaos caused by human hearts that have turned away from heaven. In throwing off the dimension of heaven and going our own way, we no longer know how to live well together. We no longer know how to live on earth in the dimension of heaven. In the Ten Commandments, God re-establishes a foundation for how human beings can live together in a heavenly way. God restores to his people the basic knowledge of how to live on earth in the dimension of his will, which is to love one another. The Ten Commandments are not rules for how to get to heaven. They are not a test paper that gives you entry to heaven if you score 85 per cent or above. They are ways of loving one another that bring the dimension of heaven to earth. As we shall see later, they are not the fullest expression of what it means to live on earth in a heavenly way, but they are foundations that begin the work of bringing heaven to earth. They are sparks that ignite the moral imagination, so that sinful human beings can begin to grasp what it means to live on earth in the dimension of heaven.

The first four Commandments deal with our relationship to Ultimate Reality, to God himself, and to the patterns of life he has written into his creation (Exodus 2:1–11). The next six Commandments deal with our relationships to other people (Exodus 20:12–17). These Commandments restore the boundaries between good and evil, the boundaries that humanity lost when Adam and Eve decided they could be the authority for moral knowledge without reference to God. The Commandments mark the boundary between trusting God and his creational patterns for humanity, and not trusting him. They mark the boundary between living in God's will and not living in his will. They mark the boundary between loving our neighbour and not loving our neighbour. They mark the boundary between living in a heavenly way or in a hellish one.

For example, the ninth Commandment is 'You shall not give false testimony against your neighbour' (Exodus 20:16). This is a law about truth-telling, honesty and openness in our communications with each other. These are essential if we are to build healthy relationships and communities. Distorting and hiding truth for self-serving ends is not God's will because it breaks bonds of trust and leads to suspicion and fear. You will know this if you have ever had a close friend or family member who has lied to you. Think of what that did to your relationship with them and to your future ability to trust and be open with them and with others. It may have taken years to heal the relationship and learn to trust again. Lies can also have destructive consequences for whole societies. In the last few years the words 'fake news' and 'post-truth' have become commonplace. It is not just internet hackers who are making up alternative 'facts', but even our politicians have less and less regard for the truth. It is no wonder that people's trust in many of our public institutions is near an all-time low.[3] The political scientist Francis Fukuyama points out that trust is an essential virtue for societies to flourish and in particular for economic growth to take place.[4] Where trust is damaged, whole cultures are filled with suspicion and fear, and become negative and creatively stagnant as a result.

Or take another example, the fourth Commandment: 'Remember the Sabbath day by keeping it holy. Six days you shall labour and do all your work, but the seventh day is a sabbath to the LORD your God. On it you shall not do any work' (Exodus 20:8–10). This is a command to acknowledge the patterns that God has woven into his creation. One of those patterns is that human beings need one day of rest in seven if we are to flourish as individuals and communities. This Commandment was in contrast to the nations that surrounded ancient Israel where the wealth of their empires was built on slaves who worked every day without rest. The community of Israel was to be different; children, servants, animals and foreigners in the land were all commanded to rest. The Sabbath was a day to enjoy human relationships without external pressures. It was a day in which people could experience a little of what it was like to be in heaven on earth. The Sabbath, therefore, marked the boundary between good and bad patterns of work and rest. When this creational order is ignored,

3 For the falling rates of trust in institutions in the USA, see <www.pewresearch.org/politics/2019/04/11/public-trust-in-government-1958-2019>, and for the UK, see <www.theguardian.com/politics/2017/jan/16/britons-trust-in-government-media-business-falls-sharply>.

4 Francis Fukuyama, *Trust: The social virtues and the creation of prosperity* (London: The Free Press, 1996).

individuals, families and communities are damaged. Workers suffer burnout, parents lose connection with their children, we become too busy and too preoccupied even to say hello to our neighbours. In our current global consumerist culture, with its emphasis on economic productivity as the most important goal, the pattern of sabbath has fast been eroded. As Sherry Turkle has noted in her book *Alone Together*,[5] computers and smartphones have blurred the boundaries between work and home, so we find it hard to switch off and give those we are closest to our undivided attention.

The Sabbath is not just about having Sunday as a quiet day; it goes far deeper than that. It is about recognizing that humans are more than work machines, that family bonds are crucial if we are to have strong communities, that for children to flourish they need time with parents who have some energy and mind-space left at the end of their working day. Some of us experienced a little of this 'sabbath' during the 2020 coronavirus lockdown. Suddenly families went for bike rides together, neighbours greeted one another in the street, families blew the dust off board-game boxes and sat down together to play. The 24/7 culture may make economic sense but the thrust of the fourth Commandment is to remind us that there is more to human flourishing than just economics, and that if we ignore the boundaries between work and rest we do so at our peril.

I hope you can see from these examples that God's laws are not arbitrary. They are foundations for bringing the loving order of heaven to earth. When human hearts are turned to these laws, we begin to see what heaven on earth looks like. They are the beginning of an antidote to the chaos of human hearts that have tried to reshape reality to suit their own selfish desires.

But giving his law is not the only doorway that God opened between heaven and earth. God also made a more permanent 'new Eden', a place where he was present on earth and where his people could once more go to meet with him.

---

5 Sherry Turkle, *Alone Together: Why we expect more from technology and less from each other* (Philadelphia, PA: Basic Books, 3rd edn, 2017). For practical advice on what to do about the invasion of media technology into our homes, see Andy Crouch, *The Tech-Wise Family: Everyday steps for putting technology in its proper place* (Grand Rapids, MI: Baker Academic, 2017).

A meeting place between heaven and earth

As Moses led the people of God through the desert towards the Promised Land, God gave them instructions to build the tabernacle;[6] a series of three tents, one inside the other so that you had to pass through all three tents to get to the middle. God said that it was within this innermost tent that he would dwell on earth among his people and speak to them (Exodus 29:42–46). However, unlike the temples of the pagan nations that surrounded Israel, the central tent did not contain a statue of God. Instead it contained the 'Ark,' a box of acacia wood overlaid with gold, within which were the stone tablets on which the Ten Commandments were written. On the cover of the box were carved two cherubim, angelic beings, their wings uplifted to enclose a space between them. That space was left empty. No idol was placed there because no man-made image could ever capture the enormity of the infinite Creator God. Rather, God said, 'There, above the cover between the two cherubim that are over the ark of the covenant law, I will meet with you and give you all my commands' (Exodus 25:22), which is why another name for that place was the 'Tent of Meeting'. Later, when the Israelites had settled in the land of Canaan, God instructed them to build a stone temple in Jerusalem to replace the tabernacle. It was constructed on the same three-layered system as the tabernacle. Just as at Jacob's 'stairway from heaven' and at Moses' 'burning bush', here was a new Eden, a meeting place between heaven and earth.

Bible scholars have noted how the structure of the tabernacle and temple reflected the world as described in the first chapter of Genesis.[7] The outer tent represents the earth, the middle tent Eden, and the innermost tent the garden, the holy of holies, where God dwelt on earth. The objects placed within the temple were also

---

6 Tabernacle means 'dwelling place' because it was the dwelling place of God on earth.

7 For example, see Gordon J. Wenham, 'Sanctuary Symbolism in the Garden of Eden Story' in *'I Studied Inscriptions from Before the Flood': Ancient Near Eastern, literary, and linguistic approaches to Genesis 1 – 11*, ed. Richard S. Hess and David Toshio Tsumura (Winona Lake, IN: Eisenbrauns, 1994), pp. 399–404.

reminders of Eden. For example, the tree-like candlestick (menorah) of the temple was a deliberate echo of the tree of life found in the middle of the garden, and the cherubim that sat atop the ark were a reminder of the cherubim with flashing swords that guarded the way back to Eden.[8] Even the words the Bible uses make this connection between the temple and Eden. The Hebrew words that describe the duties of the temple priests in the book of Numbers were the same words used to describe Adam's work in the garden,[9] and the word used to describe God 'walking' in Eden was the same word that describes his presence in the tabernacle.[10] The tabernacle and the temple were new instances of Eden, new places where heaven touched earth, new places from which the dimension of heaven, of God's will, could spread out to cover the earth.[11]

However, there was also a difference between the tabernacle and Eden, a difference brought about because of human rebellion and sin. In Eden, Adam and Eve could freely be in God's presence, because they were created to be in heaven, in God's will, on earth. When they rejected God's will, when they threw off the dimension of heaven, Adam and Eve became merely earthly beings. Because of their sin they were no longer able to be a part of heaven on earth since their hearts had turned away from the will of God. They could no longer enter the garden and speak with God freely as they had done. And the same was true for Moses and the people of Israel; the stain of their sin, of all the things they had done that had ruined God's good creation and hurt other people, prevented them from entering the new Eden of the Tent of Meeting. So God gave them a way of being cleansed from that sin so they could be in his presence again: the blood of an animal sacrifice.

---

8 Gordon J. Wenham, 'Sanctuary Symbolism in the Garden of Eden Story', from Proceedings of the Ninth World Congress of Jewish Studies, Division A: The period of the Bible (Jerusalem: World Union of Jewish Studies, 1986), pp. 19–25.

9 Numbers 3:7–8; 8:26; 18:5–6; Genesis 2:15.

10 The word 'walk' (*hithallek*) also occurs in Leviticus 26:12 and 2 Samuel 7:6.

11 The Bible Project, among many other excellent resources, has a short animated video that illustrates well this meeting of heaven and earth at the tabernacle/temple. See <www.bibleproject.com/explore/heaven-earth>.

A life substituted for a life

A few a years ago I was chatting to a student from China who had never encountered Christians before coming to the UK. He asked me to explain the story of the Bible, and when I came to describe the animal sacrifices at the temple, he asked me, 'Why blood? Why is there a need for blood? Why can't God just forgive his people and let them into his presence?' I had to think a while before I could answer, but then I saw that it was because of the seriousness of human sin and the demands of justice that there needed to be blood.

Sin is not a trivial thing. As we saw in the last chapter, sin is our broken relationship with God, which results in broken relationships with created reality and with other people. Our sin distorts God's creation and damages other people. When we break the boundaries between good and evil, we cause real hurt to other people. We cause hurt that can't just be hushed up or ignored or glossed over, hurt that can't easily be undone once we have done it. There are quite a few things I am ashamed of doing in my life. One of them is joining in bullying a boy who did nothing worse than try too hard to fit in. Somehow, he got the nickname 'Dork' and it stuck. I wasn't the worst of the name-callers, but I joined in and I didn't tell anyone to stop, or to try to call him by his proper name. I look back now and think, 'How did that affect him? How did the name-calling and the social exclusion affect him?' I will never know, but I do know it hurt. In the last few years, I have mentored many young people at L'Abri whose lives have been blighted by bullying. I have become aware of the damage done by what we often excuse as 'just having a laugh'. People who have been bullied still struggle many years later with feelings of low self-esteem and self-loathing. I know that what we did to that boy damaged the uniquely wonderful human being that God made him to be.

Even though we may not be the worst people in the world, there are many things we have done that have spoiled God's good creation and damaged other people. All of us are guilty of following in the footsteps of Adam and Eve. We have all ignored the moral fabric of reality that God has given us. Some of us do that to a greater degree and some to a lesser degree, but we all have broken relationships with God and others. We can't just say that what we have done 'doesn't really matter', or that 'they will soon get over it', or that 'it wasn't really my fault' or that 'other people do worse'. We can't even say, 'God will forgive me. It's his job.'[12] If there is to be any justice in this world, then sin must matter. It must make a difference whether we do good or evil, whether we tell the truth or lies, whether we create beauty or ugliness, whether we love others or are indifferent to them. There is a barrier between us and the dimension of heaven, a barrier that can only be crossed once the demands of justice are met and the real consequences of sin dealt with.

Of course, one way to rid the earth of evil and make it heavenly again would be to get rid of all the evil people in the world. Yet as Aleksandr Solzhenitsyn noted, it's not that simple. It's not that there are evil people 'out there' insidiously committing evil acts, and all we need do is separate them from the rest of us and destroy them. Rather, 'the line dividing good and evil cuts through the heart of every human being. And who is willing to destroy a piece of his own heart?[13]

This is God's dilemma; for the earth to be made heavenly again he would have to get rid of human beings, since we are the ones ruining his creation. Yet because he loves us, God wants to heal and restore us rather than destroy us, which is why he keeps opening doorways between heaven and earth. Yet, the price for human sin must still be paid. Justice cannot be overlooked if the difference between good and evil is to have any real meaning. So God gives a way that justice can be done, and human life saved.

God in his grace allowed the death of an animal to be substituted for the death of human beings. He gave the people of Israel a means by which they could enter into his presence, into heaven on earth. The life of an animal would be given for their life, the blood of an animal spilled to meet the blood-price for the guilt of their sin. This seems so alien to us today in our sterile twenty-first-century lives,

12 This quote is from the German poet Heinrich Heine (1797–1856).
13 Aleksandr I. Solzhenitsyn, *The Gulag Archipelago 1918–1956* (abridged edition; London: Vintage Classics, 2018), p. 75.Copyright © The Russian Social Fund, 1985.

but just imagine what it would be like to visit the temple in Jerusalem and to be literally splattered with the blood of a sacrificed animal. As the priest flicked the blood across your face and clothes with a branch, you would recognize the reality that sin is serious. You would viscerally experience that for justice to be done, a life must be given; that this animal had died in your place, so that you might go free. This ritual was enacted every day, right in the midst of the nation of Israel, so that no-one could avoid the reality of the cost of sin and the justice of heaven.

The temple marked a renewed beginning for humanity. Once again there was an 'Eden' on earth, a place where the dimensions of heaven and earth touched. There was a place where God dwelt among his people, speaking to them of his will for the earth, of how to make the earth a heavenly place. The doorway between dimensions, which had been shut when Adam and Eve ate the fruit, was open again, but only at the paying of a blood-price for human sin. God's plan was back on track. The people of Israel, with the temple at the heart of their nation, could be heavenly people again. As they took God's commands to heart, they could make their community a heavenly place to live, and by living in obedience to God's will they would demonstrate to the surrounding pagan nations what it was like to live under the rule of heaven. They would be a light that would draw the hearts of the surrounding peoples back to God.[14] Just as it was God's plan for Adam and Eve to bring heaven to the whole earth, so it was now God's plan for the people of Israel to bring the rule of heaven to the surrounding nations. God had chosen the nation of ancient Israel to fulfil the command given to Adam and Eve right back in the first chapter of the Bible: to fill the earth and order it under heaven.

The doorway is shut once more

Yet, as we continue with the story of the Bible, we see that the law written on stone tablets and the blood of animals were not enough

14 The theme of the people of Israel as a blessing to all nations is one that flows through the whole Bible. See, for example, God's promise to Abraham in Genesis 12:3.

to reunite the dimensions of heaven and earth. The nation of Israel was divided by civil war as its leaders fought one another for personal power and wealth (see 1 Kings 11 onwards). The people adopted the pagan religious practices of the neighbouring nations, even sacrificing their own children by fire to please their gods (2 Kings 17:17). The priests and prophets taught things that people wanted to hear rather than the true word of God (Jeremiah 23:16). God's chosen people kept throwing off the rule of heaven and attempting to live as if the earth was theirs to rule. Far from being a light to the world, they became a stumbling block to the spread of heaven over the earth. God continued to send prophets to call the people back to his will, but they were either ignored or killed. Over time, the temple sacrifices became mere rituals, a means to keep God happy while the people got on with living how they wanted. They had forgotten that their mission was to bring heaven to earth and, despite God's warnings, Israel would not change. So God finally brought a judgment on them.

Just as heaven was withdrawn from Eden when Adam and Eve threw off God's rule, so God now withdrew his presence from the temple in response to Israel's rebellion. The prophet Ezekiel witnessed the glory of God depart from the temple, so that the building became an empty shell rather than a touching place of heaven and earth (Ezekiel 10). As the book of Lamentations expresses it, 'He [God] has hurled down the splendour of Israel from heaven to earth' (Lamentations 2:1). In 586 BC, Jerusalem was captured by the Babylonian King Nebuchadnezzar, the temple burned to the ground and most of the people enslaved. Just as Adam and Eve were banished from the garden into the wilderness east of Eden (Genesis 3:24), so the people of Israel were taken east from Jerusalem, to be slaves in Babylon. Although a remnant of God's people later returned to rebuild the temple, things were never the same again. Those who had known the former glory wept when they saw the foundations of the new temple (Ezra 3:12). They knew God's presence was no longer there. Despite having the law of God and the blood of animal sacrifice, the people had been unable to bring heaven to earth. The doorway between dimensions was once more shut because the human heart was still closed to the will of God.

There the story of the Bible pauses for about 400 years, until the time was right for God to open a new doorway between heaven and earth. This new door was of a totally different kind. It was a door that was able both to change human hearts and meet the demands of justice for sin. It was a door that signalled a new beginning for humanity.

This doorway between dimensions was not a ladder or a burning bush. It was not found on a mountain top or in a temple. The new doorway was a person.

6
The man where dimensions meet

> 'In our world too, a stable once had something inside it that was bigger than our whole world.'
> (Queen Lucy, in C. S. Lewis, *The Last Battle*[1])

It just so happens that I wrote this chapter a week after Christmas. One of the Christmas events I love best is the Carols by Candlelight service at our local church. The beautiful 800-year-old building is lit by the warm, flickering light of hundreds of candles, while we sing the familiar carols and hear the traditional Bible readings. The Christmas story is known to billions of people the whole world over. But what is so hard to grasp, amid all the tinsel and mince pies and Christmas lights, is the truly cosmic nature of what happened that first Christmas Day. God made a new touching place between heaven and earth, not in a palace or a temple but in a child, born in a stable and laid in a cattle trough.

Theologians use the term 'incarnation' to describe the birth of Jesus. The word means 'taking on flesh', because the baby placed in that manger was no ordinary human child. He was the infinite Creator God in human flesh. He was not God just *appearing* in human form, like the gods of ancient Greece or Rome, but God become fully human. I think that is why God appeared as a baby. We might reason that it would have been far more efficient for God to have appeared as a fully grown man. Then he could have got on with things far more quickly. However, God chose to come to earth as a baby because he wanted us to understand that here was not just God

1 C. S. Lewis, *The Last Battle* (London: Puffin Books, 1964 [Bodley Head, 1956]), p. 128.

in a human form but God become utterly human. And what can be more human than a hungry, crying baby?

Here was God in flesh, with all the frailties and limitations of human life. God wasn't just playing at being human, he became fully human. Yet that baby was also fully God. As the eighteenth-century hymn-writer Charles Wesley put it, that child was 'God contracted to a span, incomprehensibly made man'.[2] He wasn't 50 per cent God and 50 per cent human, but at the same moment 100 per cent God and 100 per cent human. In the very being of that baby the dimensions of heaven and earth met, so that he was 100 per cent earthly and 100 per cent heavenly. In the language of Flatland, Jesus was the Creator of all dimensions, contracting himself to enter a two-dimensional world. He was the God that 'no-one has ever seen', made visible and knowable (John 1:18). That first Christmas morning, like the Wardrobe into Narnia or the TARDIS in *Doctor Who*, that stable held something bigger on the inside than the out. Here was a new Eden, a new tabernacle, a new temple. Those doorways had failed to truly change human hearts. They had failed to bring heaven to earth. In that stable was a totally new doorway between dimensions.

Dimensions 'torn open'

In the Bible there are four Gospels – four accounts of the life of Jesus according to those who knew him and lived with him.[3] In them you find clues as to what it meant for Jesus to be a doorway between heaven and earth. One of the first clues is revealed when Jesus is baptized. The Gospel writer Mark tells how a man called John had appeared in the Judean desert, washing in the River Jordan, as a sign of God's cleansing forgiveness, those who confessed their sins. Jesus, now a grown man, went to John to be baptized, but Jesus'

2 From Charles Wesley's hymn, 'Let heaven and earth combine', published in *Hymns for the Nativity of our Lord* (1745). For an excellent modern version of the hymn, listen to Francis Blight's rearrangement at <https://open.spotify.com/track/7DSPETTUFMEfyi9hwKXBHR>.

3 Matthew and John were Jesus' disciples and witnessed the events of his life first-hand. Mark, according to the Church Father Papias (AD 60–130), wrote down the disciple Peter's account of things. Luke, as he tells us in the prologue to his Gospel (Luke 1:1–4), wrote his account after thoroughly investigating eye-witnesses to the events he records.

washing wasn't because of sin. Rather, something else happened at that moment. Mark records that, as 'Jesus was coming up out of the water, he saw heaven being torn open and the Spirit descending on him like a dove, and a voice came from heaven: "You are my Son, whom I love; with you I am well pleased"' (Mark 1:10–11). A doorway between heaven and earth was 'torn open', and through that door came the Holy Spirit, who descended on Jesus like a dove. The Spirit of God had come from heaven to rest on this man.

When Mark describes this event he deliberately draws on the image of the Spirit of God 'hovering over the waters' (Genesis 1:2), just before the six-day work of creating order from chaos begins. Here is a new moment in creation. Just as in Genesis, when the Spirit came down to bring order from chaos, so now a doorway between heaven and earth has been torn open so that the Spirit of God can come down and bring order from the chaos of human sin. That Spirit rested on Jesus, in whom heaven and earth meet. Here was a new Eden, and a new Adam; a new human being, not steeped in sin but one with whom God was 'well pleased', because his heart was turned to God's will. We see this to be the case as the story of Jesus' life unfolds.

Following Jesus' baptism, all three Synoptic Gospels[4] tell the narrative of his temptation in the wilderness (Matthew 4:1–11; Mark 1:12–13; Luke 4:1–13). There is much that could be said about this event, but I would like to focus on how this story resonates with the temptation narrative in Genesis. Just as with Adam and Eve in the garden, the devil tempts Jesus to doubt God's goodness. The devil tries to persuade Jesus not to trust God to provide the things he needs, but to take those things for himself. For example, Jesus is hungry, so the devil tempts him not to trust God to care for him, but to use his own power to turn the stones of the desert into bread (Luke 4:3). However, unlike Adam and Eve, Jesus resists these temptations and chooses to keep trusting God and his word. History does not repeat itself because Jesus is a man in whom heaven and earth meet,

4 The Synoptic Gospels are Matthew, Mark and Luke which contain many of the same stories, with similar sequencing and wording. 'Synoptic' means 'from the same viewpoint', as Bible historians think these Gospels have a literary interdependence.

and his heart is committed to doing the will of his Father in heaven. It is after this victory over temptation that Jesus begins to preach the message that he has come from heaven to deliver: 'Repent, for the kingdom of heaven has come near' (Matthew 4:17).

Jesus' message wasn't telling people how to escape the earth. He hadn't come to tell people to abandon this world for a spiritual existence. Rather, his message was that the kingdom of heaven[5] was coming to earth, coming to be near us, coming to be among us (Luke 17:21), coming to be in our 'midst'; or, as I once heard it expressed in urban slang, 'The kingdom of heaven is coming to your 'hood.'[6] Jesus' message was that the power of heaven was flowing to earth through the doorway in dimensions that had been torn open at his baptism; but what would this power do to the earth?

The first signs of heaven coming to earth

Matthew records how Jesus went through Galilee:

> Proclaiming the good news of the kingdom, and healing every disease and sickness among the people . . . people brought to him all who were ill with various diseases, those suffering severe pain, the demon-possessed, those having seizures, and the paralysed; and he healed them.
> (Matthew 4:23–24)

These healing miracles were the first signs of the coming of the kingdom of heaven on earth. Social outcasts with leprosy were restored to health (Luke 5:12–16), a man so seriously paralysed that

5 The terms 'kingdom of heaven' and 'kingdom of God' are interchangeable. Jewish people don't like to write the word God or speak the name of God (Yahweh) because it is so holy. If writing, they might use an abbreviation such as G-d, or use a metonym like the word 'heaven' in the place of the word God. Matthew wrote his Gospel for a Jewish audience, so he uses the term 'kingdom of heaven' more frequently, whereas Luke wrote for a Gentile readership who had no such sensitivities, and therefore is happier to use the term 'kingdom of God'.

6 ''Hood' is slang for neighbourhood.

he had to be carried by his friends could walk again (Mark 2:1–12) and a man so violent that he had to be constrained by chains was restored to his right mind (Luke 8:26–39). Jesus brought a dead girl back to life and healed a woman who had suffered twelve years of continuous menstrual bleeding (Matthew 9:18–26). He raised his friend Lazarus from the dead after he was four days in a tomb (John 11:38–44) and restored the sight of a man born blind (John 9:1–12).

These were not just the 'miracles' of people with back pain throwing away their walking sticks only to ask for them back a week later. These were miracles of re-creation, miracles of the complete renewal of a broken and fallen creation. Only the re-creative power of heaven could make human cells and organs that had ceased to function begin to work again. Only the life-giving power of heaven could reverse the bodily decomposition of death. Only the renewal of God's kingdom could rewire the visual cortex of a man born blind so that he could see for the first time. These miracles were the signs of the dimension of heaven coming to earth.

As Jesus said about himself, quoting from the prophet Isaiah:

> 'The Spirit of the Lord is on me,
>   because he has anointed me
> to preach good news to the poor.
> He has sent me to proclaim freedom for the prisoners
>   and recovery of sight for the blind,
> to set the oppressed free,
>   to proclaim the year of the Lord's favour.'
> (Luke 4:18-19)

In Jesus Christ, a new doorway had opened between heaven and earth: the power of heaven was coming down to do God's will. And these miracles showed what God's will was; it was not to destroy the earth or to take God's people away to heaven. His will was to heal the earth and restore his creation. The kingdom of heaven was coming to earth to make the whole earth the heavenly place that God originally intended it to be.

Stories that explore the third dimension

As Jesus continued his ministry, he began to teach what it is like when the dimension of heaven touches the things of the earth. He mainly did this through parables. A parable is a word picture or story that makes us think and draws us towards a deeper understanding of reality. Jesus began many of his parables with the words, 'The kingdom of heaven is like . . .' (Matthew 13:24, 31), or even the questions, 'What is the kingdom of God like?' or 'What shall I compare the kingdom of God to?' (Luke 13:18, 20). In these parables Jesus uses many different word pictures to help his hearers enter into a fuller understanding of what it means for the dimension of heaven to come to earth. In one story he compared the kingdom to a mustard seed that a man planted. Although it starts as the smallest of seeds, it grows into one of the largest shrubs (Luke 13:18–19). In another story, he compared it to yeast that a woman mixes into a large amount of flour until it has worked all through the dough (Matthew 13:33).

Both these parables show how something that is almost invisible can have a profound effect on the world. A tiny seed turns into the largest of plants that provides shelter for the birds. Yeast makes a glutinous, indigestible mass of dough into delicious, wholesome bread that provides food for the hungry. This is what the coming kingdom of heaven can do to the earth. Or to use the analogy of Flatland, this is what it is like when a third dimension comes to a two-dimensional world. Something that we can't normally see is added to the world we know. This third dimension does not negate the other dimensions, but it takes them and adds to them a new depth and richness that transforms them into something far more glorious; just like the way yeast transforms ordinary flour and water into a delicious loaf of bread or a mustard seed turns into a home for birds.

However, Jesus is also realistic about the dimension of heaven. In another parable he tells the story of a man who sows good seed in a field. While everyone is sleeping, his enemy comes and scatters weeds among the wheat. When the wheat sprouts, so do the weeds

(Matthew 13:24–30). Jesus is not a romantic. He knows there is opposition to the third dimension. There are those who would undo the good work of heaven. Jesus goes on with the story to describe how the servants of the landowner ask whether they should pull up the weeds, but the owner tells them:

> 'No, because while you are pulling the weeds, you may uproot the wheat with them. Let them both grow together until harvest. At that time I will tell the harvesters: first collect the weeds and tie them in bundles to be burned; then gather the wheat and bring it into my barn.'
> (Matthew 13:28–30)

Jesus is saying that a separation of good and evil cannot be put into effect right away. Indeed, now it may be difficult to even see the difference that heaven makes to earth. But a day will come when there will be a judgment between wheat and weed. Those who have been a part of the dimension of heaven on earth will find their home in the storehouse of God, while 'everything that causes sin and all who do evil' (Matthew 13:41) will weep with regret at what they have done to God's world.

These are just some of the parables of the dimension of heaven. There are many more that work like pieces of a puzzle that fit together to give a more complete picture of what it looks like for heaven to come to earth. However, Jesus didn't just tell stories to illustrate the kingdom of heaven, he also taught his disciples what it meant for them to live in a heavenly way in the nitty-gritty of everyday life on earth.

Moving deeper into heaven on earth

Matthew tells us that Jesus 'went up on a mountainside and sat down. His disciples came to him, and he began to teach them' (Matthew 5:1–2). The fact that it was a mountain is not random. Matthew wants us to make a link between this mountain and another mountain, Mount Sinai, where God gave Moses the Ten Commandments as an antidote to the chaos of human sin. This time, however, it isn't Moses who hears God's message and brings it down to the people, but Jesus who speaks God's word directly to his disciples. Neither is it the Ten Commandments that are given, but an antidote to sin that acts far deeper in the human heart.

In the previous chapter I explained how the Ten Commandments restored the foundations of heavenly living to a people living in earthly chaos. You may have noticed that these commands are mostly expressed in the negative, as 'You shall not . . .'. A rule expressed in the negative marks a boundary between what is good and bad. For example, 'Do not touch the live wire or you will die,' or, 'Do not drive more than 50 miles an hour or you may run someone over.' The Ten Commandments mark the boundary between good and evil, between trusting God's will or taking things into our own hands. To obey them is the beginning of bringing heaven to earth. But one can ask, what lies within those boundaries? What is the positive way of heavenly living that flourishes within these boundaries? This is what Jesus taught his disciples on that mountain: a way to move deeper into the dimension of heaven on earth. Let me give you an illustration that might help us see what this means.

The L'Abri community where I live and work has its home in an old manor house, with outbuildings and seven acres of gardens. Around the property there is an ancient, lichen-covered stone wall. The wall marks the boundary of the property, but the purpose of the wall is not the wall itself. The point of the wall is that it protects the goodness of the life within it. Within the walls there is a beautiful garden where children can run and guests play volleyball and football. There are orchards of fruit trees and there are flower borders, there are woods where children build dens, and of course there are the homes where the workers and guests live. The wall keeps the cars outside on the road and out of the garden. Imagine trying to play football on the back lawn worrying that any moment a car might career across the lawn and run you down! That would severely limit your enjoyment of the game and the garden. The boundary of the wall is there because it allows life to flourish on the inside.

The Ten Commandments are like the wall. They gave a people living in chaos the basic boundaries to begin to live in a heavenly way. Now Jesus was showing his disciples what it meant to move deeper into the dimension of heaven on earth, not just live on its boundaries. Jesus said that he had not come to 'abolish the Law or the Prophets . . . but to fulfil them' (Matthew 5:17). He had not come to knock down the wall or do away with the foundations of heavenly living, but he had come to show the way to the fullness of heavenly living that the Law and the Prophets pointed to. What was that deeper way like? At the start of the 'Sermon on the Mount', as it is often called (Matthew 5 – 7), Jesus described the qualities of deeper heaven. He begins each of these with the phrase, 'Blessed are . . .' To be blessed means to grow, to flourish, to become more. These, then, are the ways that we grow and flourish in heavenly living on earth.

The deeper way of heaven on earth

Jesus taught . . .

> *'Blessed are the poor in spirit, for theirs is the kingdom of heaven'* (Matthew 5:3). In other words, the first step to moving deeper into heaven on earth is to know we need help. We must acknowledge that we need God's help if we want to live in a heavenly way. It's not something we can do in our own strength and with our own resources.
>
> *'Blessed are those who mourn, for they will be comforted'* (Matthew 5:4). To move deeper into heaven, we need to acknowledge the brokenness of the world and grieve for the sin we have done rather than pretend that we live in a utopian Disneyworld where everything is perfect.
>
> *'Blessed are the meek, for they will inherit the earth'* (Matthew 5:5). To move deeper into heaven on earth, we need to be prepared to let God guide us and not just follow our own self-centred plans.

'Blessed are those who hunger and thirst for righteousness, for they will be filled' (Matthew 5:6). Moving deeper into heaven on earth means that we long to live rightly with God, with other people, with the creation and with ourselves.

'Blessed are the merciful, for they will be shown mercy' (Matthew 5:7). The deeper way of heaven is to show undeserved goodness to those who wrong us rather than take revenge.

'Blessed are the pure in heart, for they will see God' (Matthew 5:8). Those who seek goodness, beauty and truth will find the deeper way of heaven on earth.

'Blessed are the peacemakers, for they will be called children of God' (Matthew 5:9). Heaven on earth is when we seek to heal broken relationships.

'Blessed are those who are persecuted because of righteousness, for theirs is the kingdom of heaven' (Matthew 5:10). The deeper way of heaven is being prepared to keep on doing what is right, even if it means opposition, insults and persecution.

These 'blessed' ways are how we carry out God's will on earth, how we bring the fullness of the dimension of heaven to a broken and hurting world.

Jesus continues in this sermon to give many small pictures of what this deeper way of heavenly living looks like. The examples he gives aren't meant to be new laws or rules. Rather, they are pictures that Jesus gives to fire our imagination as to what it could look like for the dimension of heaven to be present on earth. In one of his examples, Jesus reminds his disciples that the Old Testament law says, 'Eye for eye, and tooth for tooth' (Matthew 5:38). This was a law that limited justice to what was proportionate to any harm done; an eye can be taken for an eye or a tooth for a tooth. You cannot take an arm for a tooth or a foot for an eye. The law of proportionality marks the boundary to justice in a broken world. However, Jesus goes on to say:

> 'But I tell you . . . If anyone slaps you on the right cheek, turn to them the other cheek also. And if anyone wants to sue you and take your shirt, hand over your coat as well. If anyone forces you to go one mile, go with them two miles. Give to the one who asks you, and do not turn away from the one who wants to borrow from you.'
> (Matthew 5:39–42)

In a similar way, Jesus tells his disciples, 'You have heard that it was said, "Love your neighbour and hate your enemy." But I tell you, love your enemies and pray for those who persecute you, that you may be children of your Father in heaven' (Matthew 5:43–45). What exactly is Jesus saying here?

It might at first seem that Jesus is setting up another, even more exacting law than the one that God gave Moses, but it is important to remember that Jesus isn't giving us a test that we have to pass in order to get into heaven. Neither is he giving us some naive and other-worldly romantic way to live. We can all think of circumstances when it would not be right to give to someone who asks; it wouldn't be good to lend money to a gambling addict so they could continue their addiction. Rather, Jesus is showing us what it looks like to choose to move deeper into heaven, not just sit on its wall. If proportional justice is the boundary wall within which we should live, then mercy and forgiveness are essential if we are going to flourish together in the garden that is inside that wall.

Jesus is showing us what it looks like to live in a way that brings the deeper reaches of heaven to earth. He is showing us what the two dimensions of Flatland look like when they are transformed by the third dimension. He is showing a way of grace and love. He is showing us that we can make a choice, as a thoughtful act of love, to forgo our right to justice, or to pray for an enemy. When we do so, we take a step towards bringing the deeper dimensions of heaven to earth. We bring something unexpected into the world, something totally alien to the cycles of suspicion, prejudice and hatred of the sin-infected earth, something that might just make our enemies stop and wonder, 'Why did they do that?' 'Why on earth did they just do me good instead of harm?' Jesus has come from heaven to earth, not only to tell us about this deeper way of heaven but also to show us through his life what it looks like to live this way. When we bring a bit of heaven to earth, even a piece of heaven as small as a mustard seed, it can grow into great things.

On the 9 November 1987 I heard a *BBC News* interview that was one of the most extraordinary I have ever heard. The morning before, the Provisional Irish Republican Army had detonated a bomb at a Remembrance Day parade in Enniskillen. The explosion killed eleven civilians, including Marie, the 20-year-old daughter of Gordon Wilson, a local shop owner. Gordon and Marie had been watching the parade, and when the bomb exploded they were buried together beneath the rubble of a collapsed wall. Hardly able to move, they had managed to join hands and speak to each another. Marie's last words were, 'Daddy, I love you very much', before she slipped into unconsciousness and later died in hospital. The day after, Gordon sat at home still bearing the scars of his ordeal as he was interviewed by the BBC. 'The hospital was magnificent, truly impressive, and our friends have been great,' he said, 'but I have lost my daughter, and we shall miss her . . . but I bear no ill will to anybody, nor does my wife. Thankfully we are getting a grace which is helping. Very much so.' The interviewer then asked, 'When you say that you bear no-one any ill will, it must be very difficult not to feel bitter towards those who were responsible for leaving that bomb.' Gordon replied, 'I haven't really had time to think of the wider implications. I certainly don't feel bitterness. People are surprised that I don't, but I don't. I prayed for them last night, sincerely, and I hope I get the grace to continue to do so.'[7]

In the ensuing days, while loyalist paramilitaries responded with reprisals against Catholic civilians, Gordon Wilson, a committed Christian, called for forgiveness and reconciliation. He went on to become a peace campaigner, meeting with representatives on both sides of the conflict to try to stop the violence. He was later invited to become a member of the upper house of the Irish parliament.

7 See <www.bbc.co.uk/news/20257328>.

Gordon was never sure what impact his work had, but the Enniskillen bombing came to be seen as a turning point in the troubles, and it has been said that no words in more than twenty-five years of violence in Northern Ireland had such a powerful impact as those words of Gordon Wilson. Gordon had 'turned the other cheek', he had 'prayed for his enemies', he had brought a bit of heaven to earth where previously there had only been endless cycles of violence and revenge.

Love is the way of heaven

In the Sermon on the Mount, Jesus showed his disciples what it looks like for the fullness of heaven to come to earth. Jesus didn't pretend that living this way was easy. In fact, he was very realistic that we can't bring heaven to earth in our own strength, that it is impossible for sin-infected earth-dwellers to live in the way of heaven. Anyone who has ever tried to love their enemies will know what a tremendous struggle it is, but Gordon Wilson spoke of something else at work, of 'a grace which is helping'. He spoke of a power that was enabling him to do what was impossible for him to do on his own. Jesus promised this power would be given to anyone who asked (Matthew 7:7–8). Which is why, right at the heart of Jesus' sermon, he taught his disciples to pray daily to their 'Father in heaven' (Matthew 6:9–13) for the strength they would need to live on earth in a heavenly way.

Later, when the apostle Paul came to summarize this deeper way of heaven, he said that all the commands of God's law could be summed up in one rule: 'Love your neighbour as yourself . . . love is the fulfilment of the law' (Romans 13:9–10). It is love that describes what lies within the boundary of the law. The apostle John tells us that 'God is love' (1 John 4:16). Therefore, love lies right at the heart of God's will for his creation. Love is the dimension of heaven that God wants to bring to the earth. To love is to seek to be a blessing to the people and things around us, and love lies right at the heart of God's command to humanity to fill the earth and order it. God's plan was for human beings to use all the gifts he had given them *in love*, so that the two-dimensional raw material of his creation would be transformed into the glories of a three-dimensional world. It was the rejection of love by the human heart that separated the dimensions of heaven and earth, and that ruined our beautiful world. Yet, as Jesus teaches in this sermon, it is love, and only love, in all its multifaceted expressions, that will bring heaven and earth together once more. And it was the greatest act of love, which Jesus was about to perform, that would finally reunite heaven and earth so that they could never be torn apart again.

7
The cost of reuniting heaven and earth

> 'When a willing victim who had committed no treachery was killed in a traitor's stead, the Table would crack and Death itself would start working backwards.'
> (Aslan, in C. S. Lewis, *The Lion, the Witch and the Wardrobe*[1])

When I was 8 years old my parents gave me a copy of C. S. Lewis's *The Lion, the Witch and the Wardrobe.* My childhood imagination was immediately captured by the magical land of Narnia, which the White Witch kept imprisoned so that it was always winter but never Christmas. I devoured the book in a few days and then proceeded to read the entire *Chronicles of Narnia* at a similar rate. Still hungry for more, my parents gave me J. R. R. Tolkien's *The Hobbit* and then *The Lord of the Rings.* As an 8-year-old reader, Tolkien's 1,000-page epic took me rather longer to finish, but it has become my favourite book of all time and I now reread it every few years.

Lewis and Tolkien were good friends who shared a love of fairy tales and ancient myths. Tolkien, in his essay 'On Fairy-Stories',[2] reflected on the elements that link such stories. One of these was 'eucatastrophe',[3] which Tolkien described as 'the sudden happy turn in a story which pierces you with a joy that brings tears'.[4] It is that moment in a tale when evil seems to have triumphed and good has

1 C. S. Lewis, *The Lion, the Witch and the Wardrobe* (London: Puffin Books, 1959 [Geoffrey Bles, 1950]), p. 148.

2 J. R. R. Tolkien, 'On Fairy Stories' in *Tree and Leaf* (London: Allen & Unwin, 1964).

3 'Eucatastrophe' is a term developed by J. R. R. Tolkien. It is based on the word 'catastrophe', which is an event causing great suffering and damage, but modified by using the prefix 'eu' from the Greek for 'good'.

4 This quote is from a letter Tolkien wrote to his son in November 1944, published in *The Letters of J. R. R. Tolkien* (London: Allen & Unwin, 1981), letter 89.

been defeated; the hero is dead, and the quest has failed. Yet, in 'a sudden and miraculous grace',[5] there is a reversal; at the very moment evil thinks it has finally won, it has actually lost and there is, after all, a happy ending. Everyone who has enjoyed reading 'fairy tales' will recognize these moments: the stone table breaking after Aslan's sacrifice; Gandalf returning from the dead after his duel with the Balrog; Harry Potter surviving Voldemort's death curse through the protection of his mother's self-sacrifical love. Rowling was inspired by the Christian story,[6] and Tolkien and Lewis were committed Christians[7] who came to see that these eucatastrophes possessed such a peculiar power over us because they resonated with the real story of our world, with the Christian gospel. Tolkien understood that eucatastrope has its peculiar effect on us because it gives a sudden glimpse of a deeper truth to the universe than the 'chain of death', a term he used to describe the purely material processes of cause and effect. Eucatastrophe points us deeper, to 'the Great World for which our nature is made' so that, on hearing these happy reverses in a fairy-tale, we experience a 'sudden relief', like having a dislocated limb snapped back into place.[8]

As the gospel accounts of Jesus' life reach their conclusion, it appears that the whole world is indeed caught in the 'chain of death'. Jesus continued to teach, preach and heal the sick, but he met with more and more opposition from the Jewish authorities. The religious elite were frightened by his 'radical' teachings and jealous of the followers he was gaining. Fearful for their own position and privilege and incensed by Jesus' claim to be the Son of God, the Jewish ruling council seized their chance to arrest Jesus at the Passover feast in Jerusalem. They handed him over to the Roman governor Pontius Pilate, accusing him of leading a rebellion against Rome. Jesus was flogged and then taken to a small hill outside the city walls and

5 Tolkien, 'On Fairy Stories', p. 68.

6 See 'Christianity Inspired Harry Potter', *Daily Telegraph*, 20 October 2007, at <www.telegraph.co.uk/culture/books/fictionreviews/3668658/J-K-Rowling-Christianity-inspired-Harry-Potter.html>.

7 Tolkien was Roman Catholic and Lewis was Anglican (Church of England).

8 Tolkien, *Letters*, letter 89.

executed by crucifixion, a horrific death reserved for the worst criminals. John's account tells us that the Roman guards on duty stabbed Jesus in the side to make sure he was dead before releasing his body for burial (John 19:34). All four Gospels tell us that as the Sabbath was about to begin, Jesus' broken body was placed in a nearby rock tomb and a large stone rolled across the entrance. The chain of sin and death had claimed another life.

Even to Jesus' disciples it appeared that God's latest attempt to bring heaven and earth together had failed. Just like the previous doorways between dimensions, this one had also come to nothing. The way of love had been rejected in favour of a religious legalism and the desire for power. The man in whom heaven and earth met had been rejected by the people he came to save, and the selfish desires of the human heart had won. Heaven and earth were further apart than ever and the man who was the way between them had been murdered. That Sabbath day, as Jesus' body lay in the tomb, the earth remained in darkness, the light of heaven snuffed out. On the next day, the third day after Jesus was crucified, his disciples gathered together to dredge through the wreckage of their hopes and dreams. Then something extraordinary happened.

A woman burst into the room where they were gathered with the startling news: 'I have seen the Lord!' (John 20:18). The disciples must have experienced that peculiar feeling of eucatastrophe that Tolkien described: 'a catch of the breath, a beat and lifting of the heart, near to (or indeed accompanied by) tears'.[9] Could what the woman said be true?

Immediately, Peter was up and running to the tomb to see for himself. The Gospels record how Peter found the stone rolled away and the grave empty – except, as Luke tells us, for the strips of linen that had wrapped Jesus' dead body, lying neatly folded in the tomb (Luke 24:12). Luke goes on to tell how that evening, as the disciples gathered behind locked doors fearful that they too might be arrested, two of Jesus' followers returned from a nearby village. They brought the astonishing news that they had also seen Jesus alive. Jesus had

9 Tolkien, 'On Fairy Stories', p. 68.

joined them on their journey and taught them from the Scriptures, but it was only when he entered their house and broke bread at the evening meal that their eyes were opened, and they recognized who it was (Luke 24:13–35). Then, while the disciples were still arguing over what this could mean, Jesus himself was among them.

Heaven and earth torn wide open

You can imagine the tears and the joy, but also the fear. Was this a ghost from the spirit world? Or was it a phantom of their hopeful imaginations? 'Peace be with you,' Jesus said. 'Why are you troubled, and why do doubts rise in your minds? Look at my hands and my feet. It is I, myself! Touch me and see; a ghost does not have flesh and bones, as you see I have' (Luke 24:36–39). Jesus then showed them his hands and his feet where the marks of the nails were still visible in his flesh. They still found it hard to believe that it really was Jesus and not a ghost, so he asked them to give him something to eat. They gave Jesus a piece of cooked fish, and he took it and ate – and it didn't fall through his body (Luke 24:42–43). Jesus ate the fish and it went into his mouth and down his oesophagus and into his stomach. It was just as Jesus had said: he had flesh and bones. He wasn't a ghost or a hallucination. His body was solid; he was as human as they were. His body, broken on the cross of death, had been re-created. He had been resurrected from the dead, not just as a ghost or in some 'spiritual' dimension but with a body that could be touched and could eat.

This was the greatest eucatastrophe of all history, the eucatastrophe that all the eucatastrophes of fairy stories echo and point towards. Those sudden turns of events in fairy stories bring tears to our eyes because they are ripples made by the true story of the universe. The Son of God who had come to reunite heaven and earth had been killed but was alive again. The doorway between heaven and earth had not been shut but by that very death it had been torn wide open.

Matthew records how, at the moment Jesus died, the curtain of the temple in Jerusalem was torn in two from top to bottom, from heaven to earth (Matthew 27:51). This was the curtain that enclosed the most holy place where God had dwelt on earth. It was the curtain that separated a holy heaven from a sin-infected earth, but now that barrier had been torn wide open. At the very moment that the 'chain of death' appeared to have triumphed, the barrier between heaven and earth was torn in two, and the way between dimensions lay open. What had caused that tear?

You will remember that in the sacrificial system given to Moses, the barrier between heaven and earth that was the result of humanity's rebellion against heaven could only be crossed once the consequences of sin had been paid for. Which is why the high priest could only enter into the innermost place of the temple after the blood of a lamb had been spilled for his sins and the sins of God's people. God had allowed the life of the lamb to be given as a substitute for human lives, but these animal sacrifices had never been enough to get rid of that barrier. The temple curtain still remained, barring the way between heaven and earth. Now that barrier had been torn in two. What kind of sacrifice could do that? It wasn't a sacrifice that had taken place at the temple. Every day priests spilled the blood of animals, but that blood had never caused the temple curtain to tear. No, the cause of that tear in the fabric of the universe was the blood shed on a small hill outside Jerusalem where a broken body was nailed to a cross.

The very word 'tear' brings to mind Jesus' baptism when heaven was 'torn open'. Jesus' baptism was the beginning of the tear in the barrier between heaven and earth, but his death had completed that tear once and for all. What the blood of animal sacrifices could never do, the blood of Jesus had done. The man in whom heaven and earth met had given himself as a willing victim in the place of treacherous humanity. As the one 'earthly' human who had been completely faithful to God's will, his sinless life could be a worthy substitute for sinful humanity. As the 'heavenly' man, the infinite Creator God in human flesh, his death could be a sufficient and inexhaustible substitute for the sins of the entire human race. His blood could wipe away the stain of all the sins ever committed by humanity that separated the holiness of heaven from the sin-infected earth. The price of reuniting heaven and earth has been paid. The curtain separating the two was torn from top to bottom and heaven and earth could meet once more.

Over the next forty days, Jesus appeared to his disciples many times (Acts 1:3). He even appeared to more than 500 people at one time, most of whom were still alive to testify to this fact when the Epistles and Gospels of the New Testament were written (1 Corinthians 15:6). Most often he met with his close disciples and, when he did so, he did some very 'human' things. John records how Jesus once cooked breakfast for the disciples on a beach at Lake Galilee (John 21:9–14). Afterwards Jesus quietly took Peter to one side to give him words of encouragement after his earlier betrayal (John 21:15–19). At another time, Jesus did a Bible study with the disciples. He didn't 'zap' them with supernatural knowledge, but he showed them that the Jewish Scriptures foretold exactly what they had just witnessed; that the Christ would suffer and be killed, and then rise from the dead on the third day (Luke 24:46). He also taught them more about the kingdom of heaven (Acts 1:3). As he did so, things began to fall into place for the disciples. They began to remember seemingly unimportant events and things that Jesus had said, and it all began to fit together, like the pieces of a puzzle. They began to see that the cross wasn't a senseless tragedy, but that all along something other than the 'chain of death' had been at work.

There is a moment in *The Lord of the Rings* when Frodo wishes that his uncle Bilbo had never found the ring of doom and that it had never come to him, a simple hobbit from the Shire. The wizard Gandalf reassures him that there are other forces at work beyond the evil schemes of the Ring-maker. There is a deeper story to the world, in which Bilbo was meant to find the ring and Frodo to inherit it, 'And that may be an encouraging thought'.[10] What the disciples began to see from the Jewish Scriptures was that Jesus was *meant* to die on the cross. They hadn't wanted to hear it at the time, but now they remembered how before his death Jesus had said many times that he must go to Jerusalem and suffer and be killed (Matthew 16:21–23). Jesus' death wasn't merely the result of the self-serving

10 J. R. R. Tolkien, *The Lord of the Rings*, ch. 2, in *The Fellowship of the Ring* (London: Allen & Unwin, 1954).

schemes of human beings, or the final triumph of the devil in the battle between good and evil. It was part of God's plan to reunite heaven and earth. All along, other forces had been at work besides those of sin and death.

The disciples remembered that once, when Jesus was at the temple in Jerusalem, the Jewish leaders had demanded of him a miraculous sign. Jesus had answered, 'Destroy this temple, and I will raise it again in three days' (John 2:18–19). The leaders had mocked Jesus. It had taken forty-six years to build the temple, so how could Jesus rebuild it in three days? But now the disciples realized that the temple Jesus was speaking of was his body (John 2:21–22). His body was the real temple, the real touching place of heaven and earth. His body was the new Eden where heaven and earth met. It was his body that had been destroyed on the cross but raised again three days later. The temple and the whole animal sacrifice system were sign-posts to point them towards the real temple and the real sacrifice: Jesus' body and Jesus' blood. It was the willing sacrifice of the man in whom dimensions met, who was both fully God and fully human, that had opened the way between heaven and earth. The love of God had triumphed and the way was now open for the power of heaven to flow to earth. But what was that power going to do?

Death working backwards

A dualistic world view that makes an opposition between matter and spirit might assume that the power of heaven was coming to destroy the sin-infected material world and take God's faithful people to a 'spiritual' future. Perhaps this was why the disciples at first thought the resurrected Jesus was a ghost, a spirit from a non-material world (Luke 24:37). However, the Gospel accounts of Jesus' death and resurrection clearly show another direction to the power of heaven coming to earth.

Matthew records that at the moment Jesus died, when the temple curtain was torn in two, 'The earth shook, the rocks split and the tombs broke open. The bodies of many holy people who had died were raised to life.' When the power of heaven flooded out through the tear in dimensions, it came in such a sudden rush that people were raised from the dead, right there and then. But Matthew clearly states that they were raised with physical bodies, not just as souls, and that they went into Jerusalem and 'appeared to many people' (Matthew 27:51–53). Furthermore, when the disciples encountered the risen Christ for themselves, they met a physical Jesus who had a body that could be touched and that could eat food. Death had begun to work backwards. The power of heaven was coming to earth not to take the disciples away to a 'spiritual' bliss but, just as in the healing miracles of Jesus, it had come to undo all the disintegrating effects of evil and sin that were the result of humanity's rebellion against God, even the 'chain of death' itself.

The beginning of a new creation

Have you ever wondered why Jesus wasn't resurrected straight away? Why did he remain in the tomb from Friday evening until Sunday morning? It seems odd – wasn't God powerful enough to raise Jesus the moment he died? Well, the answer goes back to Genesis, chapter 1, and the creation account. In the original creation there were six days when God formed and filled the earth, followed by a seventh day on which he rested. Jesus was crucified on a Friday, which was the sixth and last day of the week. Sunset on Friday to sunset on Saturday was the seventh day, the Sabbath day of rest, during which Jesus' body lay in the tomb. It was only on the following day, a Sunday and the first day of the new week, that his body was re-created and he was raised from the dead. Why so?

Through the symbolic language of the Bible, God is telling us that a 'new' week of creation has begun. The old week of creation is over, but now something new is happening. The power of heaven is coming through the tear that Jesus made by his death, to begin a new week of creation or, rather, re-creation. The first act of creation was in the past, the day of rest was over, and a new act of re-creating the ruins of a sin-infected earth had begun. God was at work again. The power of heaven was flowing to earth, not to destroy the earth but to undo what had been defaced and destroyed by sin and to make the earth the glorious place that God had intended it to be. You can imagine the disciples' tears and joy as they finally understood God's deep, deep love for his creation. They had just witnessed the greatest eucatastrophe of all history, and heaven was on the move on earth. But then Jesus told them something they didn't want to hear.

Back to heaven

Jesus told the disciples that he was going back to heaven and would no longer remain with them on earth. You can picture their confusion and disappointment. Human sin had been paid for, the doorway between heaven and earth was wide open, and the King of heaven was in their midst. Surely now heaven would advance from strength to strength and God's will would be done over the whole earth? How, then, could the King go away? Why would he go away at just the moment when the final victory had been won?

Jesus reassured the disciples that it was for their own good that he was going back to heaven because only then could he send them someone who would help them to do the will of God on earth. Humanity needed new hearts, re-created hearts, if they were to keep trusting God and bring the loving rule of heaven to the whole earth. Jesus was going back to heaven so he could send them a 'Counsellor',[11] who would once and for all be able to change their hearts so that they obeyed the will of God (John 16:5–15). On a mountain near Jerusalem, Jesus said to his disciples: 'Wait for the gift my Father promised, which you have heard me speak about . . . you will receive power when the Holy Spirit comes on you; and you will be my witnesses in Jerusalem, and in all Judea and Samaria, and to the ends of the earth.' Then Jesus was gone, 'taken up before their very eyes' (Acts 1:4–9).

11 The term 'Counsellor' is a translation of the Greek word *paraclētos*, and is also sometimes translated as 'Advocate', 'Comforter' or 'Helper'. The word 'paraclete' was originally used in legal settings to refer to someone who helped a person in trouble with the law. It is used by the Gospel writer John to refer to the Holy Spirit (for example John 14:16) because the Holy Spirit comforts, helps and advocates for sinners who are 'in trouble' with God's law but have been set free by Jesus' blood shed for them on the cross.

Myth became fact

In the next chapter, we will explore how Jesus' resurrection and ascension point towards the eventual reunion of heaven and earth in a new creation. But before we move on, we have to ask, how do we know all this is true?

It would be easy to think of this talk of 'death working backwards' and of being 'taken up to heaven' and of 'power from above' as pie in the sky. Aren't those things the make-believe stuff of Narnia and Middle-earth? The stories of heroes who die and come back to life are found in so many myths and legends that surely the gospel is just one more example of these wishful fairy tales? We know that the real world just doesn't work that way; death is final, it brings a full-stop to our lives. Yet, as an agnostic investigating Christianity, it was the evidence that Jesus really was raised from the dead that I found to be most convincing. No matter how I tried to explain events in other ways, I kept coming back to the resurrection as the most plausible explanation. It seemed that here was an instance where myth had become fact.[12]

There are many books that go more fully into the evidence for the resurrection, but these are some of the key arguments that helped convince me that Jesus really did rise from the dead.[13]

Some people have proposed that it wasn't Jesus who was crucified, but a hastily exchanged substitute. But this just didn't make sense to me. Jesus was a public figure whose face was familiar to the Jewish authorities, and the Roman guards were far too professional to let Jesus escape and a stooge be inserted in his place.

Perhaps, then, Jesus didn't actually die on the cross but survived his ordeal to be later resuscitated in the cool of the rock tomb. Once again I just don't find this explanation believable. Could Jesus really have survived twenty-four hours of beatings, followed by a brutal

12 C. S. Lewis wrote an essay, 'Myth Became Fact', in 1944, from which I took this idea. It is published in C. S. Lewis, *God in the Dock* (London: Fount, new edn, 1998).

13 Frank Morison, *Who Moved the Stone?* (Milton Keynes: Authentic Media, 2006) was first published in 1930 but is still one of the best books on the historicity of the resurrection. For a more recent exploration of the evidence, see Gary Habermas and Michael Licona, *The Case for the Resurrection of Jesus* (Grand Rapids, MI: Kregel Publications, 2004).

flogging that would have torn his back down to the muscles and bone, followed by the slow asphyxiation and dehydration of a day spent nailed to a cross? After such extensive torture, could Jesus really only three days later pass himself off as the death-conquering Son of God? Besides, his Roman executioners knew a dead body when they saw one. They even obtained proof by stabbing Jesus in the side with a spear, which produced a 'sudden flow of blood and water' (John 19:34), a sign that he had suffered a fatal collection of fluid around the heart or lungs.[14]

Another possible explanation might be that the disciples stole Jesus' body after it was placed in the tomb and made up the stories of his resurrection, but I just couldn't see how they might carry out such a deception. A large stone was placed across the entrance to the tomb and the Jewish authorities, knowing that Jesus had talked about his resurrection, requested a guard of Romans to make sure no-one stole the body (Matthew 27:62–66). Furthermore, why would the disciples lie about the resurrection? What did they have to gain from it? None of them became wealthy or powerful through their deception but, rather, they suffered lives of persecution and hardship. All of the disciples, except one, died for their faith in the resurrected Jesus. People are prepared to die for untrue things that they believe to be true, but no-one dies for a lie they know they have made up.

Some have suggested that the resurrection was a metaphor that the disciples used to convey a general belief that even though Jesus had died, his mission would live on. However, that just doesn't make sense either. Jesus' gruesome death surely would have stripped the disciples of any romantic notions about the coming victory of God, and Jesus' public predictions about his return from the dead would have made him a liar if they did not come true. Furthermore, if Jesus' body had remained in the tomb, surely the Jewish authorities would have produced his corpse to quickly quash any rumours of a resurrection. Maybe, then, the resurrection appearances were delusions

14 The loss of blood volume and dehydration caused by crucifixion resulted in such physical stress that victims would have suffered a collection of fluid around the heart (pericardial effusion) or lungs (pleural effusion) or both. Any of these would have been terminal events for a person suspended by their arms from a cross.

on the part of the disciples. Perhaps their fanatical belief in Jesus made them hallucinate his appearances. It is here that a particular piece of evidence convinces me that the resurrection really is fact: Jesus' appearance to the disciples when the doors to the room were locked.

At first reading this might seem a classy conjuring trick, the sort of stunt a stage illusionist might perform. But the apostle John is clear that on two separate occasions the doors to the room were locked when Jesus appeared among them (John 20:19, 26). This could have been a group hallucination on the part of the disciples, which would explain how Jesus 'walked through the walls' into the room, but one fact doesn't go with this explanation: Jesus had a physical body. A hallucination of a ghost-like presence is one thing, but a hallucination of a real physical person that you can touch, hold on to, talk with and eat with, as described in the Gospels and book of Acts, is quite another. A group delusion just isn't a sufficient explanation for what the disciples witnessed in that room, let alone for Jesus' continuing appearances to over 500 people, as Paul mentions in 1 Corinthians 15:6.

The only sensible conclusion that I could come to was that the resurrection was the event that all myths and fairy tales echo, point to and long for. Only this time the hero had been raised from the dead in real history. This time myth had become fact.

8
The marriage of heaven and earth

'I shan't call it the end, 'till we've cleared up the mess.'
(Sam Gamgee, in J. R. R. Tolkien, *The Lord of the Rings*[1])

One of the things that attracted me to working at a L'Abri community is the emphasis on asking questions. Sometimes churches and Christian groups are afraid of asking questions because they consider it a sign of doubting or struggling with faith. But the truth is, we can only move deeper into reality if we ask questions. If the Bible's description of reality is true, then we can ask questions of it, confident that its truth will hold our questions. But what question we ask is crucial, because it affects the type of answer we get back. When we know the right question to ask, we are already a good way to finding true answers. As I mentioned earlier in the book, I used to think that the most important question the Christian faith answered was, 'How do I get to heaven?' Although this is a valid question, if it is the only question we ask, then it can skew our faith in a very individualistic direction. Christianity then becomes focused on what salvation does for me and we forget that God's work in history is to redeem the entire creation, not just individual human souls. As I have understood more of the biblical view of heaven and earth, I realized that the real question I should be asking is not 'How do I get to heaven?', but, 'How can I be a part of heaven coming to earth?'

When Jesus ascended to heaven and his disciples were left staring up into the clouds, two men dressed in white suddenly appeared beside them. These heavenly messengers were not floating up in the

1 J. R. R. Tolkien, *The Lord of the Rings: The return of the king* (London: Allen & Unwin, 1954).

clouds beckoning to the disciples to come up to them. Instead, they were standing on the earth, right next to the disciples, and their message was about the earth rather than heaven. They said, 'This same Jesus, who has been taken up from you into heaven, will come back in the same way you have seen him go into heaven' (Acts 1:9–11). Their message wasn't, 'One day you will go up to join Jesus in heaven,' but, 'One day Jesus will come back to earth.' Their message wasn't about humanity escaping to be with Jesus, but about Jesus coming back to earth to be with humanity. It was only a few days later that the disciples would discover the beginnings of what those angels were talking about.

The Spirit from heaven

Around ten days after Jesus had ascended to heaven, the disciples gathered in Jerusalem to celebrate the Jewish festival of Pentecost.[2] Luke records in the book of Acts:

> Suddenly a sound like the blowing of a violent wind came from heaven and filled the whole house where they were sitting. They saw what seemed to be tongues of fire that separated and came to rest on each of them. All of them were filled with the Holy Spirit and began to speak in other tongues as the Spirit enabled them.
> (Acts 2:2–4)

This sound attracted a large crowd, who were amazed to hear 'the wonders of God' being declared in their own languages (Acts 2:11).

The disciples had received the Holy Spirit from heaven, the power that Jesus had told them of (Acts 1:8). It was the same Spirit that had hovered over the waters before the first day of creation, and the same Spirit that had filled the innermost place of the tabernacle and temple; it was the same Spirit that had descended like a dove on Jesus at his baptism; and now, incredibly, that same Spirit had come from

2 The Jewish name of Pentecost is *Shavuot*, the Festival of Weeks. The word 'Pentecost' means fifty, because it is celebrated on the fiftieth day after the sabbath of Passover week.

heaven to earth to live within each of the disciples. This is what Jesus had meant when he said, 'I will ask the Father, and he will give you another advocate to help you and be with you for ever – the Spirit of truth. The world cannot accept him . . . But you know him, for he lives with you and will be in you. I will not leave you as orphans; I will come to you' (John 14:16–18). Jesus had come back to the disciples through the Holy Spirit that he and the Father had sent to live within them. They had become places where the Spirit of God was present on earth, places where heaven and earth met, places where dimensions touched. But what had the Holy Spirit come to do in them?

It was no coincidence that this giving of the Holy Spirit happened on the day of Pentecost. This Jewish festival originally celebrated the bringing in of the firstfruits of the harvest (Exodus 34:22), but by the time of Jesus it had also come to commemorate the giving of the law to Moses on Mount Sinai. As we have seen, the law showed the people of Israel the beginnings of what it was like to live on earth in a heavenly way. However, the law had been powerless to change their hard hearts and the people had kept returning to their self-centred ways. Now God was giving a new gift that could do what the law was unable to do; it would give his people new hearts that would trust God and follow his will in bringing heaven to earth. Long ago, the Old Testament prophet Ezekiel had spoken of this gift when he said, 'I will give you a new heart and put a new spirit in you; I will remove from you your heart of stone and give you a heart of flesh. And I will put my Spirit in you and move you to follow my decrees and be careful to keep my laws . . . you will be my people, and I will be your God' (Ezekiel 36:26–28).

The infinitely valuable blood of Jesus shed on the cross had done what the blood of animal sacrifices could never do. Jesus' death had paid the price for all the sins that human beings had done, were doing and would ever do in history. Through their trust in the blood of Jesus, the disciples had been cleansed from their sins and had become places where heaven and earth could meet. They had become fit places for God to dwell on earth, and he had now come to make his home within them by his Spirit (John 14:23). This Spirit could do what the law could never do; he could change human hearts from hard stone to dynamic beating hearts alive to the beauty of God's law.[3] This Spirit could bring what was dead back to life again, so that those who received him became new creations (2 Corinthians 5:17) and part of the new creation that heaven was bringing to earth. Every heart filled by the Spirit would become a place where God's will was done, a place where heaven was present on earth. Or to put it another way, every Spirit-filled person would become a temple, a place where God dwelt on earth; a place where dimensions meet.

Millions of 'mini temples' on earth

This might seem an extreme thing to say, but the apostle Paul expresses it just this way in his letter to the church in Corinth: 'Do you not know that your bodies are temples of the Holy Spirit, who is in you, whom you have received from God?' (1 Corinthians 6:19). The Jerusalem temple was where God had dwelt on earth, where heaven and earth had met. Now all those who received Jesus' Spirit would become temples, where God dwelt on earth and where heaven and earth met. This was not only true of individuals, but especially true as God's people met together in community. Jesus had taught, 'the kingdom of heaven is in your midst' (Luke 17:21), and said that 'where two or three are gathered in my name, there am I with them' (Matthew 18:20). The apostle Paul wrote, 'Don't you know that you yourselves [the 'you' here is plural] are God's temple and that God's Spirit lives among you?' (1 Corinthians 3:16). Paul understood that there was a special way in which the Spirit of God is present on earth when Christians gather together. God is Trinity: Father, Son and Holy Spirit in relationship; three in one and one in three. Other-centred love is therefore essential to who God is. Since we are made in God's image, it makes sense that we too are relational beings, made for relationships of other-centred love. It is therefore 'natural'

3 Jesus uses the personal pronoun 'he' to refer to the Holy Spirit (for example, see John 14:17 and 16:13), rather than the impersonal 'it', because the Holy Spirit is the third person of the Trinity, not an impersonal spiritual force like 'The Force' in *Star Wars*.

that God is present on earth in a special way when his Spirit-filled people meet together to do his will.

The original meaning of the word 'church' describes the people who gather, not the building. Every church, every gathering of Christians, is a temple, a place where God is present on earth, just as he was once present among the people of Israel in the temple in Jerusalem. Of course, there is one big difference between the temple and the Spirit-filled people of God; there was only one temple in Jerusalem, but there could now be hundreds, thousands, even millions of 'mini temples' of Spirit-filled people on earth. By going to heaven and by sending his Spirit back to earth, there could now be hundreds, thousands, even millions of places where the dimensions of heaven and earth met, and from where the power of heaven could flow out to re-create the earth. The plan that God had in the garden of Eden, for humanity to bring the loving order of heaven to the whole earth, was back on track. Jesus didn't stop being human when he went back up into heaven. He didn't leave his human body behind on the mountainside when he ascended. It was a fully human Jesus who sat down at the right hand of the Father, with the authority to bring the loving order of heaven to earth. Yet because he is also fully God, Jesus can send his Spirit to fill every person who is willing to trust in his cleansing sacrifice on the cross. We too can become a part of God's will to bring heaven to earth. We can become a new Eden, a new temple, a place from where the re-creating power of heaven can flow out to the earth.

First-fruits of a heavenly family on earth

But in order for the first disciples to carry out this mission over the whole earth, there needed to be many more mini temples than just the handful of remaining followers of Jesus. The feast of Pentecost not only celebrated the giving of the law to Moses, but it was also when the Jews brought the firstfruits of their harvest to the temple as a thanksgiving offering to God. That Pentecost day, when the Spirit of God descended from heaven on the disciples, they became the firstfruits of the coming kingdom of heaven on earth. But they were not to be the only fruit of the kingdom. Jesus told the disciples that once they had received the Holy Spirit, they would be his witnesses 'in Jerusalem, and in all Judea and Samaria, and to the ends of the earth' (Acts 1:8).[4] He commissioned them to 'go and make disciples of all nations' (Matthew 28:19). They were to go and tell others of what they had witnessed, that God had sent his Son as a sacrifice for the sins of the world and that all who received him would become 'children of God' (John 1:12). And this is just what they did.

The disciples took the message of Jesus from Jerusalem to the surrounding countryside, to the surrounding nations, and beyond. Wherever people believed in Jesus as their Lord and Saviour, they too received the Holy Spirit, and became mini temples, touching places of heaven on earth. As the story of the Bible continues, Jews, Samaritans, Greeks, Romans; men, women, children; free-born and slaves; all became temples of the Holy Spirit, places through which the power of heaven could flow to renew the earth.[5] This process of telling the message of Jesus, of believing in Christ and receiving his Spirit, has gone on ever since that day, down through the ages and across the globe, right to this present moment. Which means that if you, reading this book, are a follower of Jesus, then you too are a touching place of heaven on earth; you too are a mini temple in which God is present on earth and through which the power of heaven can flow to re-create the damaged world around you.

We love football in our household and there is a saying we have: 'Football is a religion . . . but Christianity is a personal relationship with God.' That is what God offers all those who will trust in him and receive the gift of his Spirit; not a religion, but a personal relationship with the Creator of the universe. Of course, this phrase can be misused to minimise the grandeur of God and make him our personal 'God-in-our-back-pocket'. Yet the wonderful truth is, that because of the cleansing work of Jesus Christ, there is now no barrier

4 The phrase 'to the ends of the earth' is not meant to be taken literally, but is a figure of speech that means 'everywhere you go'. The disciples themselves didn't travel to every corner of the globe, but since the time of the disciples Christians have travelled to every part of the earth bearing the message of Jesus.

5 The story of the beginning of the spread of the Holy Spirit is told in the book of Acts.

of sin preventing the awesome and loving Creator God from living in our hearts. God is not distant from us. As Jesus says, 'If anyone hears my voice and opens the door, I will come in and eat with that person, and they with me' (Revelation 3:20). Eating together is a beautifully intimate image of our relationship with God, because it is eating at a kitchen table that is at the heart of being family together. When we receive the Holy Spirit, we become part of God's heavenly family on earth, with the mission of bringing the loving order of heaven to every part of our world.

How does the story end?

Before we think about what it means here and now for us to be mini temples of heaven on earth, I would like to describe how the story of heaven and earth ends. It is important to know where we are headed if we want to journey there.

In Revelation, the last book of the Bible, the apostle John records a series of visions he had while in prison on the island of Patmos. The imagery of his book is complex and it is written in a Jewish literary style that is unfamiliar to us today,[6] so his message needs careful and thoughtful interpretation. However, as his visions reach their conclusion, John receives a clear picture of how the story of heaven and earth will end.

> Then I saw a new heaven and a new earth, for the first heaven and the first earth had passed away, and there was no longer any sea.[7] I saw the Holy City, the new Jerusalem, coming down out of heaven from God, prepared as a bride beautifully dressed

6 This highly stylized form of literature, known as apocalyptic, is used in various places in the Bible, notably Revelation and Daniel, but also parts of Isaiah, Joel and Zechariah. It uses symbolic imagery, including symbolic numbers, to speak about events, particularly the final events that will occur when God returns to judge evil and rule over the earth.

7 This is an example of apocalyptic literary symbolism. In the Old and New Testament, the sea is used as a symbol of fallen nature, in rebellion against God. For example, in Matthew 8:23–26, the storm-tossed waves attempt to drown Jesus and his disciples while they are in a boat. The absence of sea in the new creation isn't meant to be taken literally but, rather, to say that, in the new creation, all nature will be brought under God's good and loving order.

for her husband. And I heard a loud voice from the throne saying, 'Look! God's dwelling-place is now among the people, and he will dwell with them. They will be his people, and God himself will be with them and be their God. He will wipe every tear from their eyes. There will be no more death or mourning or crying nor pain, for the old order of things has passed away.'

He who was seated on the throne said, 'I am making everything new!'

(Revelation 21:1–5)

The marriage of heaven and earth

When I first encountered John's final vision of heaven and earth I almost fell off my seat. I had expected him to say that human history would end with the earth destroyed and God's people taken up to heaven. Instead John saw a new heaven and a new earth, and the Holy City coming down from heaven to be on earth, like a bride beautifully dressed for her husband. The final reality he describes is a far cry from the Neoplatonic dream of humanity escaping the material world for a 'spiritualized' heaven. What John sees is not the end of the physical creation, but the physical creation renewed and fulfilled by the grace of heaven. The language is one of a marriage; a marriage of dimensions, a marriage of heaven and earth. In the language of Flatland, John sees the completion of the two-dimensional by the glory of the third dimension. Just as we have seen throughout the Bible, God's plan is not to destroy his creation but to redeem it by bringing heaven and earth together.

But if the earth isn't going to be destroyed, why does John write about a *new* heaven and a *new* earth? The Greek word used here for 'new' is the word *kainos*.[8] This word is not used to describe something brand new but, rather, something that had been *re*newed or made new again. For example, it would be used to describe an old dilapidated mansion that has been redecorated and restored to its original glory. This sense of the earth and heavens as *re*newed

8 The word *kainos* is also used in other places in the Bible that describe these end times, such as 2 Peter 3:13.

resonates with other biblical words that describe God's action towards his creation, such as *re*demption and *re*storation. So a more accurate way of expressing what John saw in his vision is a *renewed* heaven and a *renewed* earth, a heaven and earth made new again, restored to how God intended them to be. John saw nothing less than the final marriage of heaven and earth. God's plan to make the whole earth a heavenly place had finally been achieved through the death, resurrection and return of Jesus Christ to earth.

But doesn't the Bible say the earth will be destroyed by fire?

If the story of the Bible ends with a new heaven and earth, why do so many people believe that it tells of a final battle between heaven and earth that results in the final destruction of our world? This 'Armageddon'[9] is not only the focus of some Christian groups but has also found its way into popular culture, such as Neil Gaiman and Terry Pratchett's book and TV series *Good Omens*, where an angel and a demon become friends and work together to prevent the end of the world because they have come to love it and its people.[10] From a dualistic perspective, the fiery destruction of the earth and an escape into heaven makes perfect sense, since we can only achieve spiritual perfection once we escape our material nature. These dualistic ideas can then become a lens through which any Scripture that talks of the end times is viewed. Indeed, at first sight, some scriptures appear to support the idea that the earth is destined to be destroyed by fire. Back in Chapter 1, we touched on a passage in the apostle Peter's second letter, where he writes: 'But the day of the Lord will come like a thief. The heavens will disappear with a roar; the elements will be destroyed by fire, and the earth and everything

9 Armageddon is named in Revelation 16:16 as the place where 'the kings of the whole world' gather on 'the great day of God Almighty'. The Hebrew name may mean 'mountain of Megiddo', but like much of the book of Revelation it is probably a symbolic reference to other biblical texts, such as the defeat of Gog on the 'mountains of Israel' in Ezekiel 39:1–4, rather than intended to be an exact geographical location.

10 Neil Gaiman and Terry Pratchett, *Good Omens* (London; Victor Gollancz, 1990). TV series (Amazon and BBC TV, 2019), directed by Douglas Mackinnon.

done in it will be laid bare . . . That day will bring about the destruction of the heavens by fire, and the elements will melt in the heat' (2 Peter 3:10, 12). Elsewhere, there are verses that talk about the Lord Jesus 'revealed from heaven in blazing fire with his powerful angels' (2 Thessalonians 1:7), and describe God as 'a consuming fire' (Hebrews 12:29). However, as we have seen from John's vision in Revelation, and as the whole biblical narrative witnesses to, God's plan is not to destroy the earth but to renew it. Even in the passage I quoted above, Peter finishes by saying: 'But in keeping with his promise we are looking forward to a new heaven and a new earth, where righteousness dwells' (2 Peter 3:13).[11] Why, then, does the Bible use the image of consuming fire?

Burning up the bad to leave the good

Fire, in the Bible, is not merely a destructive phenomenon but also a purifying one. Where fire does destroy, it is not just for the sake of destructiveness but, rather, to burn up the bad in order to reveal the good. Both Old and New Testaments speak in many places about fire in this sense as a refining fire.[12] For example, when Paul talks about leaders and teachers in the church he says: 'their work will be shown for what it is, because the Day [when Jesus comes again] will bring it to light. It will be revealed with fire, and the fire will test the quality of each man's work. If what has been built survives, the builder will receive a reward. If it is burned up, the builder will suffer loss' (1 Corinthians 3:13–15).

God loves his creation. In Neoplatonic dualism, there is something inherently wrong with creation itself, but in the biblical narrative we are told seven times in the first chapter of Genesis alone that God's creation is good. And God does not destroy the good. However, his good creation has been distorted by human sin. In the Christian world view the problem is not the physical creation itself but the physical creation when it is twisted and distorted out of shape by

11 The same Greek word *kainos* (to be made new) is used in this verse too.

12 For examples, see Numbers 31:22–23; Psalm 66:10; Isaiah 48:10–11; Jeremiah 9:7; Daniel 12:10; Malachi 3:2–4; 1 Corinthian 3:13; 1 Peter 1:7.

selfish human hearts. So the fire that Jesus brings with him when he returns is not a destroying fire, but a refining fire. It is a fire that will burn up evil and all its distorting effects, in order to restore God's creation to its intended glory. This will include the glory of created nature, of plants and animals, of rivers and mountains, oceans and forests. But it will also include the glory of human civilization.

John's vision in Revelation is not of a garden but of a city (Revelation 22:1–22). In Chapter 3 we saw that human history and civilization were part of God's good plan for his creation, part of the unfolding of his glory. Sin has defaced and distorted everything, but the structural goodness of God's creation has never been lost. Human history has been both glory and ruin. The refining fire that Jesus brings will not destroy everything but, rather, it will clean away the encrusted filth of evil to expose the glory of human civilization as God intended it to be. This fire will not destroy all the achievements of humanity and return us to a 'primitive' state in the garden. Instead, it will 'bring to light' (1 Corinthians 3:13) what is truly worthwhile in the works of human civilization. Everything that is meaningless and worthless, everything that is destructively self-centred and only fit for refuse, will be exposed for what it is and will be burned up. Everything that is evil will be finally and fully destroyed, including the devil and all his allies, while everything that is meaningful and worthy and true and beautiful and good will be purified and revealed by this fire and seen for what it is. Just imagine all the wonders of human invention and imagination, of science and art and technology and creativity, all cleansed from the self-serving effects of sin to be revealed in all their glory. Everything on earth that has been touched by the dimension of God's will, by the dimension of heaven, will remain. As John tells us, 'the kings of the earth will bring their splendour' to that city (Revelation 21:24).

However, John's vision is not just a city, but a garden city. It is a city with a river flowing through the middle (Revelation 22:1), with fruit-bearing trees (Revelation 22:2); and yes, the new creation will have animals too (Isaiah 11:6–9). People often ask whether there will be animals in heaven. Perhaps it is just a question that concerns pet-lovers, but the answer is an emphatic 'Yes!' Although these passages use figurative language, it makes sense that if God's will is to reconcile to himself 'all things, whether things on earth or things in heaven' (Colossians 1:20), then this 'all things' must include the creatures of God's good earth that he has given into our care as stewards of his creation. For they are part of his glory and were created to sing his praise (Psalm 148:7–12).[13]

The emperor is coming to heaven's colony on earth

Another passage that some people use to support the idea that the earth will be destroyed while we escape to heaven, is found in Paul's letter to the Christians in Thessalonica. He writes:

> For the Lord himself will come down from heaven, with a loud command, with the voice of the archangel and with the trumpet call of God, and the dead in Christ will rise first. After that, we who are still alive and are left will be caught up together with them in the clouds to meet the Lord in the air. And so we will be with the Lord for ever.
> (1 Thessalonians 4:16–17)

At first sight, these verses appear to be saying that when Jesus comes again we will ascend into the clouds to be with him and go up to heaven.[14] However, as the New Testament theologian Tom Wright explores in *Surprised by Hope*,[15] Paul is describing Jesus' return using images that connect with other events in the Bible. The trumpet call is a reference to the trumpet blast that was heard when God descended from heaven to the top of Mount Sinai (Exodus 19:16–19). The words 'caught up in the clouds' bring to mind an Old Testament

13 For the Reformers' views on this question, see Chapter 7, 'Redemption: Hope, love and restoration' in Philip J. Sampson, *Animal Ethics and the Nonconformist Conscience* (London: Palgrave Macmillan, 2018).

14 Some Christians link these verses in 1 Thessalonians to the idea of the rapture, a future event when Jesus returns to capture up believers, both living or dead, to meet him in the air and take them to heaven, before victoriously returning with them after a period of tribulation has passed on earth.

15 Tom Wright, *Surprised by Hope* (London: SPCK, 2007). See ch. 8.

prophecy that speaks of 'one like a son of man, coming with the clouds of heaven' (Daniel 7:13), a prophecy that Jesus applied to himself (Matthew 26:64; Mark 13:26; Luke 21:27). Wright argues that Paul is blending these biblical allusions with a Roman custom, whereby the citizens of a colony went out to meet a visiting emperor before returning with him to their city. What Paul is saying is that when Jesus comes again it will be like the emperor coming to take up residence in a city. Only this time it will be the true Emperor of heaven who will return to his earthly colony, and his people will go out to meet him and welcome him into their city with joy.

The overwhelming witness of the Bible is that human history will not end with the destruction of the earth but, rather, with its renewal. The healing miracles that Jesus performed – the dead that rose to life the moment that Jesus died on the cross; the physical body of the resurrected Christ that could be touched and that could eat food; the giving of the Holy Spirit at Pentecost to those on earth who trust in Jesus; the vision of the renewed heaven and earth that John saw and that Peter testifies to – all these show that the kingdom of heaven is not coming to destroy the earth but to restore it. God has not, and will not, give up on the good creation that he has made. And neither will he give up on human beings, creatures uniquely made in his image whom he loves and has chosen to bring the rule of heaven to the whole earth.

When Jesus comes again his refining fire will cleanse the earth from every kind of evil and restore God's creation to the glory that he purposed for it from the beginning of time. The mess of suffering and brokenness, of evil and sin, will once and for all 'be cleared up'. God will dwell on earth among his people, and his people will carry out his will throughout the earth, so that human history is once more a display of the marvellous wisdom of God. The dimensions of heaven and earth will be joined in a joyful marriage, never to be torn apart again. A glorious new age will begin.

But what will it be like in this new creation, and what will we be doing there for eternity?

Part 3

TAKING PART IN HEAVEN ON EARTH

9
What on earth will it be like in heaven?

> Of course it is different; as different as a real thing is from a shadow or as waking life is from a dream.
> (C. S. Lewis, *The Last Battle*[1])

There is an idiom that says, 'you can fall off a horse on either side'. This is true when we think about heaven. I discovered on that flight to Warsaw that I didn't want to go to heaven because all the images I had been given seemed so insipid. Heaven was supposed to be my deepest joy and longing but being a disembodied soul floating for eternity in a spiritualized heaven seemed so unattractive compared to this earthly life that I live within a physical body. But one can also fall off the horse on the other side. We can make heaven into a personal paradise where all our best holiday fantasies come true but with no room for God in it. What, then, will it actually be like 'in heaven'?

As we have seen in the last few chapters, the focus of the Bible isn't on us going to heaven, but on heaven coming to earth. When Jesus comes again, it will not be to destroy the earth and take us to heaven, but to heal and restore the earth with the power of heaven. In fact, the future that the Bible speaks of is not 'heaven' at all, but a united heaven and earth, a new creation. This new creation has already begun, but it will not reach its fulfilment until the day Jesus returns. When he does, everything that is good and true and beautiful about this earthly life will be restored and completed by the dimension of heaven, and the whole earth will be a heavenly place. As I saw what

1 C. S. Lewis, *The Last Battle* (London: Puffin Books, 1964 [Bodley Head, 1956]), pp. 153–154.

the Bible actually said about heaven and earth, I began for the first time to get excited about this future. However, I still found myself wondering what it would be like to be there, and what I was going to be doing for eternity.

Not less, but more than this world

Jesus said that he came, not to give us a smaller 'spiritualized' version of life, but to bring us life in all its fullness (John 10:10). One of the difficulties we have when we think about the new creation is that it is hard for us earth-dwellers to imagine what that fullness might be. Whether it was because of the influence of dualistic theology or because of paintings depicting fluffy cloudscapes, I could only imagine the life to come as less than this physical world. Other people might imagine it to be a future in which we get to do all the things we love doing without anyone else there to interrupt our fun. What, then, will a 'fuller' reality be like? A good place to turn to for clues is to explore what the Bible says about Jesus' body after he was raised from the dead, since in Jesus' resurrection the new creation had begun to break through into our world.

The disciples, like us, had difficulty grasping what a new creation meant, so that when they first met the risen Jesus they expected him to be a ghost with less solidity than the dimensions of the earth around them (Luke 24:37). It was only when Jesus made them touch him, and when he ate some fish and it didn't fall through his body, that they began to see that the final reality was not less solid than this world but more solid than earthly matter. In fact, it was because of this solidity that Jesus could appear among the disciples even though the doors to the room were locked (John 20:19; 20:26).

Most of us would assume, like the disciples did, that Jesus could appear in the locked room because he had a ghost-like form that could pass through the solid barrier of the walls. However, Jesus clearly proved to the disciples that he wasn't a ghost but had a body that was just as physical as their bodies. How, then, could he move through the walls? Perhaps Jesus could dematerialize and materialize at will, but that sounds more like the teleportation machine of the

USS Enterprise than the Jesus of the Gospels. An explanation that is more in line with our thinking about dimensions is that Jesus could move through the walls of the house not because he was insubstantial, but because compared to the weightiness of his resurrected body the barrier of the walls was insubstantial.[2] Even modern physics has affirmed that the material world isn't quite as solid as we usually assume, discovering that around 99.999999999996 per cent of the space of every atom is occupied by a non-material electron field. Jesus' resurrected body was already part of the final reality of a united heaven and earth. He could move through walls because the earthly dimensions around him were as thin shadows compared to the weighty dimensions of his resurrected body. As I thought about this, I began to see that heaven is not a shadow realm compared to the earth but, rather, the other way round; the earth is shadow-like compared to the glorious marriage of dimensions that awaits us when heaven and earth are united.

Our earlier visit to Flatland might help us understand this better. You remember that Flatland is a world of only two dimensions, length and width. The circles, triangles and squares of Flatland live in flat houses with two-dimensional walls and doors. When a Sphere from the three-dimensional world of Spaceland first visited Flatland, he spoke to the Flatlanders from the third dimension, from 'above' Flatland, but all the Flatlanders experienced was a disembodied voice. The Sphere appeared invisible to the Flatlanders because they could only see in two dimensions. So they thought that Spaceland must be less solid than their world. Now, imagine the Sphere entered Flatland. He could appear inside the rooms of the Flatlanders' houses, even though the doors to the rooms were locked because he could enter the rooms from above, from the third dimension. The Flatlanders might think that the Sphere could move through the walls of Flatland because he was less solid than the two dimensions of their world, but they would be wrong in this assumption. The Sphere could appear behind locked doors because he was more solid

2 I believe this idea has its origins in the writings of G. K. Chesterton, but I first heard of it through my friend Ellis Potter, pastor, philosopher, author and itinerant apologist.

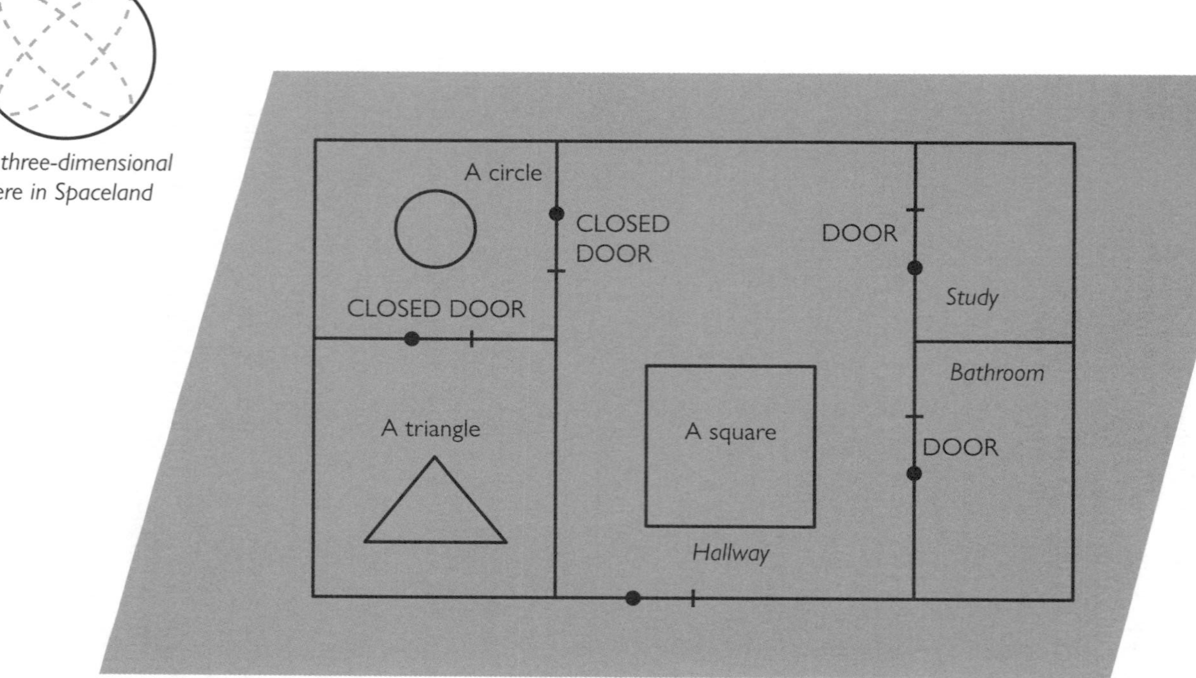

Figure 4 **From Spaceland, the Sphere can see into every room in the house or appear in each room even though all the doors are closed**

than the dimensions of Flatland. It is the three-dimensional nature of the Sphere that allows him to move 'through' the Flatland walls.

The shadowlands

It is not easy for us to imagine a reality that is more solid than this world, but I have found several of C. S. Lewis's books extremely helpful in this regard. In *The Great Divorce*[3] and *The Last Battle*,[4] Lewis develops the idea that the earth is a 'shadowland' compared to the solid reality of the life to come. In the first of these he takes an imaginative journey through hell and heaven. When Lewis first arrives in heaven his attempts to walk on the lush grass prove painful. He writes, 'The grass, hard as diamonds to my unsubstantial feet, made me feel as if I were walking on wrinkled rock . . . A bird ran across in front of me and I envied it. It belonged to that country and was as real as the grass. It could bend the stalks and spatter itself with the dew.'[5]

What Lewis is doing is inverting the normal images we have of earth and heaven. The world view of spirit–matter dualism sees heaven as a spiritual realm, free from the material substantiality of the earth. But Lewis, in line with Scripture, shows us that the final reality of the new creation is not less substantial but more substantial than this world. Earthly visitors to the new creation cannot at first walk on the grass because it is so much more solid than they are. Each blade forms a sharp spike that painfully projects into the soles of the visitor's feet. Even a small bird of the new creation is more substantial than a new visitor because it belongs to that country. It is only as Lewis moves deeper into heaven that he can finally walk without discomfort.

The same idea is found in *The Last Battle*, the final book in Lewis's Chronicles of Narnia. As the story reaches its conclusion, the central characters witness the end of Narnia, a land they have come to love so much. With heavy hearts they pass through a magical doorway

3 C. S. Lewis, *The Great Divorce* (London: Geoffrey Bles, 1946).

4 Lewis, *The Last Battle*.

5 C. S. Lewis, *The Great Divorce* (London: Fount Paperbacks, 1997 [1946]), p. 17.

into another world and begin to walk through the country that lies before them. As they do so they begin to recognize features of woods and hills, and distant mountains that remind them of the old Narnia. Then they realize that this land is exactly like Narnia, only different. There are more colours and things seem bigger and grander, more like the real thing than in the land they have left behind. At last Lord Digory realizes that the old Narnia

> was only a shadow or a copy of the real Narnia which has always been here and always will be here ... You need not mourn over Narnia ... all of the old Narnia that mattered, all the dear creatures, have been drawn into the real Narnia through the door, and of course it is different; as different as a real thing is from a shadow or as waking life is from a dream.[6]

The weight of glory[7]

Lewis never intended his stories to be exact representations of the future that awaits us when the new creation is fulfilled.[8] But in them he does capture the wonderful truth that our final destiny is not an other-worldly spiritualized heaven, but a new creation in which everything that matters from this earth is restored to how God intended it to be. Everything will become more itself, more real and more meaningful. It will not be a shadow world that is less weighty than the dimensions of the earth, but the earth completed and fulfilled, the earth glorified by the dimension of heaven.

In fact, weighty is just what glory means. The Hebrew word used in the Old Testament for glory is *kavod*, which literally means

---

6 Lewis, *The Last Battle*, pp. 153–4.

7 This is the title of a sermon preached by C. S. Lewis in 1941, which is published in C. S. Lewis, *Essay Collection: Faith, Christianity and the church* (London: HarperCollins, 2000), pp. 93–106.

8 Lewis's description of the 'real Narnia' is very helpful in understanding the physical reality of the new creation. Of course, like all imaginative attempts to capture a bigger truth, it is not perfect in its analogy with the relationship of creation to new creation. One could argue that in the Last Battle, the old Narnia is destroyed before the characters enter the real Narnia. However, Lewis never intended his stories to be direct allegories of the Christian faith but, rather, to take us 'farther in and farther up' towards a deeper understanding of biblical truth.

'weight' or 'heaviness'. So the glory of something is the solid weightiness of its reality. Heaven has more glory than the earth because it has the weightiness of being the dimension where God's will is done. The earth has its own glory: the weightiness of the goodness of the created dimensions of time and space. Yet when the dimension of heaven comes to earth, it is like adding a third dimension to Flatland, or like adding time to the spatial dimensions of my dining table. These added dimensions do not negate the existing dimensions or squash them into non-existence. Rather, they add new meaning and depth, a new weightiness to the reality that is already there. They add glory, the glory of all things being exactly as they were purposed to be in the good and loving will of God.

In the New Testament, both the writer of the letter to the Hebrews and the apostle Paul talk about this world as a 'shadow' when comparing it to the more solid realities that are coming.[9] Paul encourages new Christians in Colossae not to let anyone judge them by what they eat or drink, or how they keep religious festivals or the Sabbath day, because these things 'are a shadow of the things that were to come; the reality, however, is found in Christ' (Colossians 2:16–17). What Paul is saying is that the food laws, festivals and celebrations of the Old Testament, even the Sabbath day, are shadows cast by a deeper, fuller reality. It is not that such earthly laws and festivals are unimportant or wrong, but they aren't the real thing. They are signposts that point us towards something far more solid in which they find their fulfilment. In fact, they point us towards the man in whom heaven and earth meet, to Jesus Christ himself. Jesus is not more shadowy than these earthly laws and festivals because he is from heaven. He is the solid, glorious heavenly reality that casts these shadows on the earth. The fulfilment of these religious practices is found in the weighty reality of Jesus Christ and in the kingdom of heaven that he is bringing to earth. Let me just give you one example of how this works.

9 In Hebrews 8:5 the author says that the tabernacle sanctuary is 'a copy and shadow of what is in heaven', and in 10:1 writes that 'The law is only a shadow of the good things that are coming – not the realities themselves.'

Paul tells the Colossian Christians that the Sabbath day is a shadow of Christ. What does he mean? As we saw in Chapter 5, the Sabbath was the day on which God invited the people of Israel to lay down their burdens and experience rest. They were to rest from their work and trust God to meet their needs rather than rely on their own efforts. It was a day when they enjoyed something of what it had been like to be with God in the paradise of Eden. Paul, however, tells the Colossians that the Sabbath was only a shadow of Jesus Christ. He is the fulfilment of the Sabbath. He is the real Sabbath to which the Sabbath day points us. It is not ultimately in a day of the week, but in the deeper reality of a trusting relationship with Jesus, that we find the rest that Adam and Eve enjoyed in the garden of Eden. This is just what Jesus himself said: 'Come to me, all you who are weary and burdened, and I will give you rest' (Matthew 11:28). It is in trusting Jesus that we experience the rest of heaven on earth. We will still be working in the new creation, as I will talk about later in this chapter. Work and rest are not opposites in the Bible, although they have often come to be so in our sin-infected creation. The opposite of 'rest' in Scripture is the 'anxious striving to making life work in our favour' that comes when we choose to 'go it alone' without God.[10] When we turn back to a trusting relationship with Jesus, we begin to experience the rest of knowing that our loving heavenly Father works in all things 'for the good of those who love him' (Romans 8:28).

Will there be marriage in heaven?

As earth-dwellers, we can barely begin to grasp the joys of what it will be like to be a part of this wonderful future. All too often we turn the glory of the new creation into something that is flat and boring and unattractive. On that flight to Warsaw I realized this is what had happened to me, but Jesus also encountered people who made a similar mistake. Once some members of a Jewish religious sect, who didn't believe in a bodily resurrection, tried to catch Jesus

10 I take this from Genesis 3. Following Adam and Eve's rebellion against God, their work, rather than being the 'restful' work of doing God's will on earth, becomes sweaty, frustrating, painful toil (Genesis 3:17–19).

out by posing him a conundrum about a woman who had been married and widowed seven times in this life. 'At the resurrection', they asked, 'whose wife will she be?' Jesus replied, 'At the resurrection people will neither marry nor be given in marriage; they will be like the angels in heaven' (Matthew 22:23–33).

Because of dualistic thinking, people have often taken Jesus' words to mean that there will be less than marriage and less than sexuality in heaven. They argue that since sexuality is an earthly function of our bodies, we must become asexual beings when we are in heaven. But this is to reduce the dimension of heaven to something that is less than this world. If we understand heaven as a dimension that expands the earth, then we should expect that earthly marriage, and even earthly sexuality, will be completed and fulfilled in heaven. This would be in line with other parts of the Bible where we are told that marriage is a signpost to the deeper reality of the love that Jesus Christ has for his people (Ephesians 5:32). When heaven and earth are united, there will not be less than marriage but more than marriage. As an earth-dweller I can hardly comprehend what this will mean, but perhaps it will be that the trusting, faithful, joyful and fruitful relationship that is earthly marriage (at its best) will be so expanded and fulfilled by the intimate relationship we enjoy with God in the new creation that all our relationships will share in this same quality of love, while not in any way diminishing the special relationship we have had with the person we were married to in this life.

I am not suggesting that we will be polyamorous in the new creation! That would be to reduce heaven to earthly terms. Human sexuality is a wonderful earthly reality, but it points beyond itself. The joyful, ecstatic, intimate, other-centred and fruitful sexual union experienced on earth points to something even deeper and more fulfilling in the new creation. It ultimately must point to the eternal joy of being welcomed right in the heart of the joyful, other-centred, life-giving love of the Trinity and being with other people who are filled by that same love.

As Flatlanders, we can only just begin to imagine the edges of heaven on earth, but we are called to expand our imaginations in a heavenly direction rather than shrink heaven to fit the earth. The future that awaits us when Jesus comes again will be a wondrous glory. It will not be less than this world but the expansion of dimensions, as the weightiness of heaven, the dimension where God's will is done, completes and fulfils the earth. In the end we will find that we do not love heaven because it contains the things of this life, but that we loved this life because it has contained the things of heaven. When the new creation is fulfilled we will echo the words of the Unicorn in *The Last Battle*, who says about the new Narnia, 'I have come home at last! This is my real country! I belong here. This is the land I have been looking for all my life.'[11]

Made for joy

As I began to understand this glorious future that awaits us when Christ returns to earth, I found that I began to long for the fulfilment of the new creation. But I still had a big question: what would we actually be doing there – for eternity? The simplistic answer I had been given in church was that we would worship God for ever. In my impoverished two-dimensional imagination, I saw this as being like a never-ending church service or a ceaseless praise and worship-song session. But as I thought more about the biblical story from creation to new creation, I saw a thread woven through the whole narrative that gave me a clue as to what we will be doing in heaven on earth.

The first thing we will be doing is enjoying it, because this is what God made us for. The Westminster Shorter Catechism states that 'Man's chief end is to glorify God and enjoy him forever.'[12] God made human beings to enjoy being with him in the garden of Eden and to take joy in carrying out his will of making the whole earth a heavenly place. It is humanity's rebellion against heaven that has cut us off from much of this joy. When Jesus brings heaven to earth and God once more dwells right in our midst, that joy will be completed

11 Lewis, *The Last Battle*, p. 155.

12 The Westminster Shorter Catechism is a reformed confession of faith drawn up by the Westminster Assembly in 1646–47, which forms a basis of belief for most of the Presbyterian Church. This is the answer to question 1 of the catechism, 'What is the chief end of man?'

and fulfilled. All evil and sin and death will be banished once and for all so that there will no longer be any barrier between heaven and earth, and between us and God.

In our earthly lives now, our experience of God is incomplete. Even if we are Christians and mini temples where the Holy Spirit dwells on earth, our relationship with God is not yet fully what it will be when Jesus comes again. Even though those who receive God's gift of the Holy Spirit have already become a part of the new creation, the fullness of that new creation will not be realized until Jesus returns. Now we know the joy of being with God 'through a glass darkly' (1 Corinthians 13:12, KJV), as if we are looking at him through a grimy dirt covered window. When Jesus comes again we will be with God 'face to face' (1 Corinthians 13:12). This is why the apostle John, in his vision of the new creation, 'did not see a temple' in the holy city. A building would only separate us from God's presence. Instead, 'the Lord God Almighty and the Lamb are its temple' (Revelation 21:22), because they will be dwelling with us, right in our midst.

It is hard to comprehend what this will be like, but if, as the apostle John tells us, 'God is love' (1 John 4:8), then knowing God face to face is nothing less than being welcomed into the very heart of love itself; the love that the three persons of the Trinity have shared with one another from eternity to eternity; the love that overflowed in the creation of the universe; the love that is present in all the good things we have ever enjoyed; the love that is the source of all the love that we have experienced in our relationships on earth; the love that we begin to experience as we trust Jesus and his care for us. This is the never-ending joy that God offers us through the death of his Son Jesus Christ.

An eternal crown

The second thing we will enjoy about the new creation is being with one another. The Christian vision of the future is not a place where we become amorphous souls or become absorbed into the oneness of the divine being. The new creation is a place where we will be our true selves, more ourselves than we have ever been. In this life on earth we have always been distorted and diminished by the effects of sin, but in the new creation we will be fully restored to the person God created us to be. We will be more ourselves than we have ever been because we will be fully healed and restored by the love of God. The love of God in Jesus Christ begins to heal our wounds now on earth, but that process will only be complete when Jesus comes again to wipe every tear from our eyes, as Revelation 21:4 promises. And all the people who are enjoying this future with us will also be healed and restored so that they are more themselves than they have ever been. When we meet someone in the new creation, I imagine we will say, 'Ah, now I see the glory of who God created you to be! What a wonder you are! What a joy to know you!' Together we will be so filled with the love of the Trinity that to share love with one another will be perfect joy. We each will receive many times what we give, and the joy of heaven on earth will increase for ever.

When the Bible talks about the life to come, it often refers to a 'crown' that awaits those who have faithfully served the Lord Jesus during their lives on earth (1 Corinthians 9:25; 1 Peter 5:4). We might imagine this crown to be like the golden pocket watch that employees are sometimes given as a reward for long service in a company. However, if you read carefully, you see that the crown we will receive in the new creation is not gold – it is other people. The apostle Paul describes the Thessalonian Christians as 'the crown' in which he will glory in the presence of Jesus when he comes again (1 Thessalonians 2:19), and he calls the Christians in Philippi, 'My joy and my crown' (Philippians 4:1). These are people with whom Paul had shared his life and people whose lives had been transformed by his teaching, encouragement and love. Our crown, then, is not a lump of gold, it is the joy of being in eternal relationship with the people whose lives we have blessed with the love that we have received from God.

I sometimes imagine the new creation as being a place where we will meet people, perhaps people we have forgotten that we ever met, and they will say, 'You may not remember, but you said something that changed my life, that gave me courage when I was full of despair,' or, 'The kindness you showed me gave me hope that there could be goodness in the world,' or, 'The way you forgave me when I hurt you showed me the reality of God's love,' or, 'That artwork you made really helped me see something true about the world.' Then someone else might come up and say, 'You won't know this, but because of your love for that person, they were able to show me kindness in a similar way, and that released me from my guilt which had been a destructive burden all my life,' or, 'Because you encouraged them, they in turn were able to support me, without which I would never have made that important discovery'; and so on, and so on, and so on. Our crown, our glory, will be all the unseen ways we have been a part of the kingdom of heaven in the everyday acts of love and service we have done on earth. These acts will have been like ripples of the glory of heaven on earth, and who knows where such ripples will end?

The joyful work of the new creation

So the new creation will be a place of never-ending, ever-increasing joyful relationship with God and with one another, but what will we actually do there? The answer is that we will reign over creation! At the beginning of the Bible story, we were created to work alongside God in ruling as stewards, caring for his creation and its creatures. He gave human beings the dignity of being co-creators with him in extending the boundaries of Eden until the whole earth was a heavenly place. It is this plan that Satan derailed when he persuaded humanity to throw off the dimension of heaven. As we pursued our own self-centred plans for God's creation, our work became an anxious striving to protect our own interests rather than the rest-filled work of being a part of God's will on earth.

Yet God never abandoned his plan for human beings to be stewards of his creation. Rather, he sought to restore humanity to the dignity of this work by opening doorways between heaven and earth, and finally by uniting heaven and earth through the death of his Son. When Christ went back up into heaven, he sat down at the right hand of God, from where he now reigns over creation until all things are brought under the loving rule of heaven (Ephesians 2:9–11; 1 Corinthians 15:25). As we shall see in the last chapter, it is this mission of bringing heaven to earth that is the work that Christ calls us to be a part of now on earth. But why should this work end when Jesus comes again? Why should we not continue the work of making the new creation an ever-increasing 'display of the marvellous wisdom of God . . . and the profound meaningfulness of our task in the world'?[13] The Bible tells us that in the new creation we will be given the wonderful honour of reigning with Christ over his world (2 Timothy 2:12; Revelation 22:5).

I had been taught that when Jesus comes again he will instantly bring the whole earth to a state of absolute perfection; in a flash everything will be restored and the whole creation completed. But this left me with a question: if everything would instantly be made perfect, what would there be for humans to do, other than keep very still lest we mess up the perfection? As I understood the flow of the whole biblical narrative, I began to wonder whether the new creation might not also be a dynamic reality rather than an instantly perfected static one. After all, the original creation was dynamic in the sense that God created Adam and Eve to care for the earth and make more of it as they brought it under the loving order of heaven. Why wouldn't this also be true of the new creation? Why would we not continue to be co-workers with God in the ever-increasing glory of the new creation? Why would we not continue to care for the creation and its creatures, to invent and discover and design and build and express creativity, and take eternal joy in doing all these things and sharing all these things with other people made in the image of God? The way we will worship God in the new creation is not by singing hymns for eternity, but by being a part of the continuing unfolding of God's glory in the wonders of his creation.

Some years ago, I was talking to a Christian who worked on the Great Barrier Reef, the world's largest coral reef, off the coast of Australia. He was a marine biologist and his job was to find ways of restoring parts of the reef that had been damaged by tourism and

13 Al Wolters, *Creation Regained: Biblical basics for a reformational worldview* (Grand Rapids, MI: Eerdmans, 2nd edn, 2005).

pollution. As we talked about the new heaven and earth, he asked me, 'What will I be doing there?' I replied, 'You will be doing the same thing you are doing now, continuing to care for the Great Barrier Reef.' You see, he was already following Christ's calling to be a part of the restoration of God's creation by attempting to heal the damage that human beings had done to one of the most beautiful marine habitats on the planet. When Jesus comes again, it may be that he will not 'magic' the Great Barrier Reef better, but instead invite people like this marine biologist to be his co-workers in restoring the reef to the glory of what it was meant to be.

Indeed, God will invite all of us to use our skills and gifts and experiences and passions to restore his world to the glory he intended for it, and then to increase that glory in a never-ending story. And of course, in the new creation there will not be the frustration of seeing the good work we do fall apart again or being undone by our sins or the sins of others. Our efforts will be meaningful and satisfying, and part of the eternal joy that God has destined for us since before the beginning of time.

Before I saw what the Bible really taught about the new creation, I had no desire to go to heaven because it seemed such a boring future. But now I long to be in the fulfilment of heaven on earth. I long for a fully restored relationship with God in which I am welcomed into the joy-filled love of the Trinity. I long to be healed and renewed, and to enjoy restored relationships with other people filled with God's love. I long for a restored relationship with the created world and for the meaningful, satisfying work of being a part of the growing reality of heaven on earth. Who could ever be bored with those things? We will not be bored even for one second, but like the characters in *The Last Battle*, we will find that we are a part of the Great Story, 'in which every chapter is better than the one before'.[14]

14 Lewis, *The Last Battle*, p. 165.

10

What on earth happens to us when we die?

> I believe in the resurrection of the body and the life everlasting. (Apostles' Creed[1])

So far in this book, I have focused on the big picture of what God is doing to bring heaven and earth together rather than the individualistic 'personal salvation' focus that can easily distort our expectations of heaven. However, we are important to God as individuals. He does not treat us merely as machine-like cogs in his plans. So having understood the big story of the Bible, I now want to explore how our individual stories interact with what God is doing in human history.

Before joining L'Abri Fellowship I worked as a hospice doctor and for four years had the uncomfortable privilege of being with dying people every day of the working week. It was a most amazing education. I learned from my patients what was and what was not important about life here on earth. But it was also challenging to be forced to confront every day the question that most of us put off thinking about for as long as we possibly can: 'What happens to us when we die?'

Hope of an afterlife

Despite our present 'secular age', many people still have a hope that this life is not all there is. A 2018 survey of the UK population found that despite declining religious belief, 43 per cent of people still

1 The Apostles' Creed is one of the earliest statements of Christian belief. There is good evidence that it dates from at least the fourth century AD, although what it teaches goes right back to the writings of the early Church Fathers, the apostles and the Bible itself.

believe in life after death.[2] In the USA the figure is more like 80 per cent and is increasing.[3] A similar Canadian study rather surprisingly found that millennials (18–29-year-olds) are more likely to believe in an afterlife than older generations.[4]

Many religions share a belief that the human soul survives beyond death. They often affirm a circular life cycle in which we begin as an eternal soul, enter a physical body when we are born, and return to be a soul once more when we die. Some of the major Eastern religions teach the doctrine of reincarnation, whereby after death a soul is reborn in a higher or lower earthly form depending on whether the person has lived a good or bad life. I have heard that some Tibetan Buddhist monks feed stray dogs that gather around the monastery walls because it is taught that bad monks are reincarnated as dogs. What is interesting is that whether the belief in immortality is part of a religion, a vague hope or a technological dream, all these visions of the afterlife share a dualistic view of a human being; they all believe that we are made up of an eternal soul (or mind) and a temporary body. The soul (or mind) is our real self, whereas the body exists more as a vehicle that we inhabit during our time here on earth.

Body–soul dualism

I have discovered that Christians often unconsciously also share this split between body and soul. At a recent L'Abri discussion, a guest asked, 'Is just my body female, or is my soul female too? Will I still be female in heaven?' It is a really good question, but you can see that what underlies it is a dualistic view of humanness; the 'real me' is my soul, and my body, with its gender, is just a shell that I inhabit on earth. On that flight to Warsaw I discovered that I too had a similar dualistic view. I believed that when I died I would leave my body behind and become a disembodied soul in a non-material heaven. It

2 See <www.brin.ac.uk/news/?tag=british-social-attitudes-surveys>.
3 See <www.nbcnews.com/better/wellness/fewer-americans-believe-god-yet-they-still-believe-afterlife-n542966>.
4 See <https://nationalpost.com/news/canada/millennials-do-you-believe-in-life-after-life>.

was this that made heaven seem unattractive or at the very least unimaginable to me as an embodied earth-dweller, but a few years after I prayed that God would help me long for heaven, I saw the answer. It had been staring me in the face all along: 'I believe in the resurrection of the body and the life everlasting.'

This phrase is part of the Apostles' Creed, one of the earliest statements of Christian belief. I had been saying it every Sunday as part of the church service I attended. For some reason, that Sunday I suddenly saw the words as if for the first time: 'I believe in the resurrection of the body.' It was the word 'body' that stood out. This ancient creed didn't say 'the resurrection of the soul' or 'spirit', but 'body'. I began to realize that Jesus' resurrected body wasn't just a means of proving to the disciples that he was alive. Jesus didn't dispense with his resurrected body when he went back to heaven. The disciples didn't witness Jesus' soul ascend to heaven leaving his lifeless body on the earth at their feet. Jesus went up to heaven *with* his resurrected body, because he was the firstfruit of the united heaven and earth. His body was evidence that the new creation is a very different future from the popular understanding of the afterlife. His body was evidence that in the new heaven and earth, we too will have bodies for eternity, just as the resurrected Jesus does.

This is the conclusion that the apostle Paul came to when he wrote to the Christians in Philippi that 'we eagerly await a Saviour from [heaven]' who will 'transform our lowly bodies so that they will be like his glorious body' (Philippians 3:20–21). Or, as he puts it elsewhere, 'Christ has indeed been raised from the dead, the first-fruits of those who have fallen asleep[5] . . . For as in Adam all die, so in Christ all will be made alive. But each in turn: Christ, the first-fruits; then, when he comes, those who belong to him' (1 Corinthians 15:20–23). Paul saw Jesus' resurrected body as the firstfruits of the transforming power of the Holy Spirit. When Jesus comes again that same power will raise all those who had received the gift of that Spirit, so that they too will have bodies like his; bodies not just of the earth but of heaven also. Jesus' resurrected body was proof

5 'Fallen asleep' is a synonym for died.

that the final destination for humankind was not the Neoplatonic dream of being a soul floating free from the confines of the material world but, rather, the Christian hope of a restored creation in which we will continue to be embodied beings in a united heaven and earth.

The goodness of bodies

The trouble with the idea of being a soul in heaven is that I have always known myself as an embodied being and everything I have ever known about life has been through my body. All the good I have ever known – from a kiss to a glass of chianti; from the sun on my face to the feeling of a hot shower on my back; from hearing words of comfort to sights of beauty – all these things I have known in a body. What I saw that Sunday in the statement, 'I believe in the resurrection of the body', was the unique, outrageously wonderful hope that the risen Christ gives: we will continue to be embodied beings in the life to come.

In this digital age it is easy to downplay the importance of our bodies. Media technologies enable us to do business, socialize and even have 'sex' in virtual worlds. Some social analysts predict that soon we won't need to be bodily with other people any more. Yet it was interesting to observe the effects of social distancing practices that were imposed during the 2020 coronavirus epidemic. Initially there was a frantic period when everyone learned to use video-conferencing platforms to enable them to keep working from home and to stay in contact with friends and family. However, very quickly reports of 'Zoom fatigue' began to appear, a feeling of exhaustion and anxiety associated with taking part in multiple video calls.[6] It appears that meeting in cyberspace drains our energy as we struggle to communicate without cues like facial expression, tone of voice and body language. Not being able to make eye contact or share a social coffee break all reduce the satisfaction of the contact, sapping us of life rather than energizing us. In this technological age we may

6 See <www.bbc.com/worklife/article/20200421-why-zoom-video-chats-are-so-exhausting>.

be tempted to overlook the importance of our bodies, but if we do so we ignore one of the most crucial aspects of our humanness.

One of the reasons we want to do without bodies is that in this broken world our bodies frequently let us down. We age and grow weary, we suffer ill health and physical deformities, we struggle with liking how our bodies look and even with the sex that we are born with. Yet imagine being perfectly at ease with your embodied being and that body being restored and healed and renewed so that it is absolutely as you were meant to be. Imagine knowing that your body is as much you as your inner being; in fact, that the inner and outer is perfectly integrated in one unique joyful person. Imagine being with other embodied beings and that you are all filled with the ever-increasing joy of the love of God that you share with one another. Imagine being in a physical world where everything that mattered in this world is more its real self. This is how it will be when Jesus comes again.

I have a friend who is a season ticket holder and huge fan of Arsenal Football Club. He travels to every home game in his wheelchair because he is paraplegic, having suffered a high spinal cord injury in his mid-twenties. We were once discussing having restored bodies in the new creation and I said, 'I can't wait to play football with you when we get there.' 'You'd better watch out,' came his quick reply, 'I'm a real hacker.'[7] Whether we will be hacked or not while playing football, the new creation will not be less than we have known in this life, but all the best of this life healed and fulfilled and glorified, including our bodies. That is truly something I can look forward to.

Created to care for the material world

The 'resurrection of the body' also gives Christians a uniquely positive view of the physical world that is unlike almost any other world view. We are not just visiting the world of matter as a temporary resident while we learn spiritual lessons and then escape

7 A 'hacker' is someone who fouls you by 'hacking' your legs out from under you.

to a higher realm. Neither are we here merely as the product of random forces of time and chance set in motion by the Big Bang. Nor is the diversity of the physical world an illusion that we need to be freed from by realizing that true reality is an undivided oneness of being. We are here in a physical world, with physical bodies, because that is exactly where God purposed us to be and where we shall be in the future. The creation account in Genesis tells us that God made us to be embodied beings who live within the physical dimensions of a created earth. His purpose in making humanity physical beings was because he wanted us to care for the physical creation and its creatures. The mission God gave humanity in the garden of Eden was not an other-worldly spiritual quest, but the command to care practically for the material world that he had made. In the Christian world view, having bodies is not a barrier to spirituality but how we live out our spirituality in a physical world.

Of course, the earth we see now is not the heavenly earth that God intended it to be. Humanity has thrown off the dimension of heaven, and the earth is now a distorted and misshaped version of what it was created to be. Many religions conclude that the problem is matter itself, and that we can only truly be spiritual when we escape this physical world. The Christian world view is very different from this. Christianity takes seriously the brokenness of the world, but it does not conclude that matter is inherently evil. Rather, it conclues that something has happened which has distorted and twisted the physical creation. The Christian solution therefore is not the destruction of the material world, but its redemption, so that it is restored to its created goodness. We see the firstfruits of this restoration in the healing miracles that Jesus performed, in Jesus' bodily resurrection from the dead, and in the giving of his Spirit to dwell within the bodies of those who trust in him. We will see its fulfilment when Jesus comes again and the dead are raised to live in a renewed heaven and earth.

This emphasis on the original goodness and final restoration of the material creation gives Christians a unique reason to care for the world in which God has placed us. The earth is not our temporary residence while we wait to escape to heaven, but the place where God created us to live and the place we will share for eternity with all of God's creatures. It is when Christianity has been influenced by the dualistic idea that matter itself is bad that care for God's creation has been neglected and the earth abused. Some Christians have used the argument that in the end 'everything will burn' to excuse the pillage of the earth's resources and the destruction of its habits for the 'benefit' of humanity. However, when Christians have understood the true biblical emphasis on the final redemption of the created order, and God's commission to humans to be stewards of his creation, they have been at the forefront of caring for the earth and its creatures. Today we know William Wilberforce best for his campaign to end human slavery, but he was also a founding member of what became the Royal Society for the Prevention of Cruelty to Animals. Like many other Christian reformers of the time, his faith compelled him not only to social action but also to a deep concern to care for all of God's creation.[8] Today there are many organizations, such as A Rocha[9], that encourage Christians to take seriously their God-given role as stewards of the earth. It is hope in the resurrection of the body and the restoration of the physical creation that gives impetus to such works.

The Resurrection at Cookham Churchyard

A few months ago I visited the Tate Britain art gallery and saw a painting that shocked me in its vivid depiction of this Christian hope of resurrection. On a huge canvas, the British artist Stanley Spencer had imagined the moment of the resurrection occurring in the churchyard of his boyhood village of Cookham.[10] The painting shows men and women, even couples together, many dressed in smart suits and dresses, literally bursting out of their graves. It is full

8 If you want to read more on these reformers' attitudes to animals, I recommend Philip J. Sampson, *Animal Ethics and the Nonconformist Conscience* (London: Palgrave Macmillan, 2018).

9 See <www.arocha.org/en>.

10 See <www.tate.org.uk/art/artworks/spencer-the-resurrection-cookham-n04239> or <www.bbc.co.uk/programmes/p00j5pml> for a short video exploring the painting with archive footage of Spencer himself talking about his work.

of small 'earthy' details; one woman rising from her grave stops to smell a flower, while in another place a newly resurrected girl thanks her 'alive' friend for placing a wreath on her tomb. Beneath the rose-covered church porch sits Jesus, and behind him stands God the Father who lays a hand lovingly on Christ's hair.

What shocked me about this painting was the way Spencer had captured the sheer physicality of the moment when Christ returns to earth. This was no Neoplatonic dream of souls but an earthy resurrection of real people. Indeed, many of the figures in the painting were modelled on Spencer's friends and the artist even included an image of himself emerging from a book-shaped tomb. In his painting, Spencer has captured the exuberant joy of the moment when Christ brings heaven to earth and death can no longer keep people in their graves. It echoes the words of Paul when he wrote of the day when 'the creation itself will be liberated from its bondage to decay and brought into the freedom and glory of the children of God' (Romans 8:21). This is the wonderful future that awaits those who will receive the gift of new life that is made possible through Christ's death and resurrection. But this still leaves a question . . .

What happens to us between our death and Jesus' return?

If resurrected bodies and a new creation are the future that awaits us when Jesus returns to earth, what happens in the meantime? If we die before Jesus comes again, what happens to us between our death and Jesus' return? There are two answers I am going to give: a traditional answer and a more modern one. In the end they come to the same thing, but both are worth thinking about.

The traditional Christian answer is that, at death, the soul of a person who has received Christ's gift of new life goes to be with him in heaven. Our body remains on earth and suffers decay, rotting in the grave until all that is left is dust, for 'dust you are and to dust you will return' (Genesis 3:19). What it will be like to be a soul in heaven we don't exactly know. However, we can receive comfort from Jesus' words to the repentant thief who was crucified alongside him:

'Truly I tell you, today you will be with me in paradise' (Luke 23:43). In the next chapter we are going to think more about Jesus' promise to this thief, but for now I want to point out the reassurance that these words give us about what it will be like to be a soul in heaven.

The word 'today' implies that the thief will be with Jesus as soon as he dies. There will be no period of sleep or unconsciousness before he is in heaven. Although the Bible does in places use the language of 'falling asleep' to describe those who have died trusting in Christ (John 11:11; 1 Corinthians 15:6), this language is used to emphasize that they will one day 'awake' at the resurrection rather than to indicate they are in a state of unconsciousness. The words 'with me' signify that the thief will be in a conscious relationship with Jesus, and the word 'paradise' implies that being with Jesus in heaven will be an experience of pure joy. Paradise was used at that time to describe the peaceful delight of being safe in the palace garden of a king. Jesus is therefore reassuring the thief, and us, that if we trust in him, then the moment we die we will be safe in a joyful, loving relationship with God such as Adam and Eve enjoyed in the garden of Eden. However, as we have seen, this is not the final destination that awaits us after death. The souls of the dead wait in the bliss of heaven for that glorious day when Christ brings heaven and earth together. Just as heaven and earth are reunited, so will the souls of the dead in heaven be reunited with their bodies in the new creation. Our final destiny is to be embodied human beings in a new heaven and earth.

The biblical understanding of the soul is not the same as the dualistic view. In dualism the soul is the real me and the body merely the vehicle I inhabit during my earthly life. However, in the biblical world view, we are integrated body-soul beings in which our bodies are just as much us as our souls. The soul is not so much *the* key component that can be isolated out as the 'real me' but, rather, one of the qualities that makes up our humanness.[11] The body quality of

11 Greek thought, which has influenced much of Western thought, has a greater emphasis on the substances of which things are made. Hebrew thought is more interested in the qualities that things possess. For an interesting comparison of the two, see Thorleif Bowman, *Hebrew Thought Compared with Greek* (New York: W. W. Norton and Co., 1970).

our humanness allows us to inhabit space and interact with the physical world within which God has placed us. The soul quality of our humanness is approximately what today we would call our psycho-emotional person. In Scripture, the soul can be filled with anguish (Psalm 31:7) and grief (Psalm 31:9), or rest (Psalm 23:3; 62:1) and joy (Psalm 35:9). The soul longs for the good things of God (Psalm 119:20) and for the presence of God himself (Psalm 42:1–2), but the soul is not our true self and the body merely a vehicle we inhabit. God created us as integrated, embodied souls and that is also what we shall be in the new creation.

At death, the body quality of our humanness decays because it is not yet fully part of the new creation. Our bodies are still subject to the frustration and groaning of the created order while it awaits Jesus' return (Romans 8:22–23). But the new life that Jesus gives by his Spirit preserves beyond death the souls of those who have received Jesus' gift of new life. As we have seen, when someone makes a decision to trust Christ, they are no longer just on earth but have also become a part of the dimension of heaven. So when the body dies and decays, the soul or spirit continues to live on in heaven. Yet even though the souls of the dead in heaven are in the conscious joy of the presence of God, they are also longing, together with all creation, for the day when Jesus reunites heaven and earth. Then they shall be reunited with their bodies and be complete human beings again. In the beginning, God created us to be embodied beings in heaven on earth, and our final destiny in the new creation is to be embodied beings in a renewed heaven and earth. God's plan for his creation will not be thwarted.

Time in heaven and on earth

I said above that souls 'wait' in heaven for the day when Christ returns to earth, which might sound like we will just be passing time there until the second coming. But, of course, to use the term 'wait' is to assume that earth and heaven share the same quality of time. This is not necessarily the case. Earthly time is part of God's creation through which he gives order to the world he has made and a matrix of sequence to our lives on earth. It is also affected by our rebellion against God, so that earthly time can drag or we can 'waste' time. However, if heaven is the dimension of God's will, then it is not bound by earthly time, just as it is not bound by earthly space. It has a different quality of sequence that is hard for us earth-dwellers to imagine. We tend to think of heaven as endless earthly time, so that when Jesus promises 'eternal life' to those who trust in him (John 6:40), we take him to mean 'never-ending' life, which to us earth-dwellers might sound like it would drag after a while. However, eternal life is much more than that; as we have seen in the last chapter, it is to participate in the fullness of life that is found in the love of the Trinity. So, rather than imagining heaven as the conscious passing of earthly time, it might be more accurate to describe it as time fulfilled, completed and thickened by ever-deepening relationships of meaning and joy. The time of heaven is more the kind of time we experience when we are so engrossed in a good conversation or some meaningful pursuit that we don't even notice earthly time passing. In heaven, time does not drag or fly away. Time is always unhurried, in which each moment is meaningful and precious and has its proper place.

There is another way of looking at all this, which might seem more 'sci-fi time travel' than the traditional Christian view but I think nonetheless worth mentioning. As we have seen, when someone who has received Jesus' gift of the Holy Spirit dies, they are no longer a part of earthly space and time but their soul continues to exist within the dimension of heaven. From heaven they can 'go' to the moment when Christ comes again without having to 'wait' for time to pass on earth, since they are outside earthly time. So it may well be that when we die, we 'time travel' in the blink of an eye from the moment on earth when we died to that time when Jesus comes to earth again and the dead are raised. Time will continue to pass on earth. On earth it may be a year from our death, or a 100 years or 10,000 years, but because we are outside time in heaven, there is no time for us between breathing our last and being resurrected. We will, on that very day, be with Jesus in the joyful fulfilment of the new creation.

I don't think it really matters whether we believe the traditional view or the 'time travel' one. What is important is the sure hope that Christians have beyond this life. Death is not the end, but a joyful future awaits all those who have received the gift of eternal life through Jesus Christ. That future is not to be a disembodied soul floating among pink fluffy clouds, but the joy of being reunited with our resurrected body in a new heaven and earth.

Is the resurrection of our bodies really possible?

As earth-dwellers we might quite rightly ask how the resurrection of a person's body is possible. It is easier to believe in the immortality of a non-material soul than a resurrected physical body. How can God raise bodies that have been in the grave for centuries or even millennia so that no physical remains exist? What if someone has been cremated or died in a fire? What if all the cells of our body have decayed in the grave and then been reabsorbed from the soil by plants that have then been eaten by animals? Parts of us could be in a million different places, shared between a thousand different organisms. How could God bring someone's body back together again?

The new Christians in Corinth also had such questions, asking the apostle Paul, 'How are the dead raised? With what kind of a body will they come?' (1 Corinthians 15:35). To answer their question, Paul uses the analogy of a seed. When you sow you do not place the mature plant in the ground but a tiny 'simple' seed. Yet God has created the seed so that it grows into a plant that is far more complex and glorious than the seed. I have a small vegetable patch where I plant a few seeds every spring. To me all the seeds look roughly the same, so I always find it amazing, even miraculous, that these tiny identical dry, black specks grow into delicious lettuce, rocket, spinach or carrots.

Paul says that our earthly bodies and resurrected bodies are like the relationship of seeds to plants. There is a continuity between seed and plant, just as there is a continuity between our body here on earth and our bodies in the new creation. Yet there is also a difference: 'The body that is sown is perishable, it is raised imperishable; it is sown in dishonour, it is raised in glory; it is sown in weakness, it is raised in power; it is sown a natural body, it is raised a spiritual body' (1 Corinthians 15:42–44). Our resurrected bodies will not be less than our earthly bodies, just as a plant is not less than the seed it comes from. Our risen bodies will not be physicality-minus, but physicality-plus, just as Jesus' resurrected body was physicality-plus. When Jesus unites heaven and earth, we will not just have earthly bodies but bodies that are also part of the eternal, imperishable, glorious dimension of heaven. They will not just be natural bodies, but 'spiritual' bodies; not because they are made of some non-material 'spirit' matter, but because they are filled with the empowering Spirit of God, the same Spirit that was given at Pentecost as the firstfruits of the new creation.

So we don't need to worry about what happens to the specific atoms of our bodies after we have died. The God who not only transforms seeds into plants, but who in the beginning created from nothing every atom of the entire material universe, is more than capable of recreating our bodies at the resurrection of the dead. It is his power that holds every molecule of the universe together so that it does not disintegrate into chaos (Colossians 1:17) and on the last day will bring every molecule together to 'transform our lowly bodies so that they will be like his glorious body' (Philippians 3:21). But what happens if I am alive on earth on the day that Jesus returns? What kind of a body will I have then?

Changed in the twinkling of an eye

Strangely enough, this is a question that some of the first Christians also asked, particularly those from more dualistic Greek-speaking backgrounds who struggled with the idea of a bodily resurrection. The apostle Paul reassures them that neither those who have died nor those who are still alive when Jesus returns will miss out, but that ' in a flash, in the twinkling of an eye . . . the dead will be raised imperishable, and we [those still alive] will be changed. For the perishable must clothe itself with the imperishable, and the mortal with immortality' (1 Corinthians 15:51–53). Or, to put it in dimensional language, when Jesus returns, the perishable earthly bodies of those who are still alive will be clothed with the imperishable dimension of heaven, so that they become earthly-heavenly bodies, just like the glorious resurrected bodies of those who have died. This is the wonderful future that Christ makes possible through his death and resurrection.

The philosopher Luc Ferry writes in *A Brief History of Thought* that human beings, as distinct from animals, are the only creatures on this earth who are conscious of their mortality. We know that one day we will die and so will all the people we love. Thus, he says, it is the constant struggle of human existence to stop ourselves from being overwhelmed by this knowledge that is 'disturbing and absurd; almost unimaginable'.[12]

The bodily resurrection of Jesus Christ tells us a different story. It tells us that we need not fear death. Death is an alien that has invaded our world through sin but, because of Christ, death will not have the last laugh. There is a power at work stronger than death, a power that raised Jesus from the dead, a power that will raise us at the last day to be a part of God's glorious new creation. Through Christ's death and resurrection, death itself has lost its sting; it has been 'swallowed up in victory' (1 Corinthians 15:54–55).[13]

---

12 Luc Ferry, *A Brief History of Thought: A philosophical guide to living* (New York: HarperCollins, 2011), pp. 2–3.

13 Paul quotes from the Old Testament prophets, Isaiah 25:8 and Hosea 13:14.

11
Who on earth can take part in heaven?

> 'Jesus, remember me when you come into your kingdom.'
> Jesus answered him, 'Truly I tell you, today you will be with me in paradise.'
> (Conversation between the thief on the cross and Jesus, Luke 23:42–43)

The thief on the cross is one of my Bible heroes. We aren't told his backstory, other than that he was crucified alongside Jesus for crimes against the Roman state. Yet this criminal recognized something about the 'man' on the cross next to him that led him to put his trust in Jesus. What I admire about him is his courage; the tremendous courage to admit that the way he had lived his life up to that point had been all wrong; the courage to admit that he needed help, and the humility to ask for that help. Of course, you could think that it doesn't take much courage to ask for help when you are nailed to a cross with only a few hours left to live, but my experience has shown me otherwise.

People often ask me whether, during my time spent working with the terminally ill, I saw many 'death-bed' conversions. The answer is that I saw surprisingly few, even though, like the thief on the cross, the hospice patients were facing imminent death. What I came to understand is that it takes tremendous courage to change your whole view of life in your last few weeks on this earth. It takes a special kind of courage to admit that for 50, 60, 70 or 80 years you have been missing the key ingredient of life and ignored a relationship that would have changed everything. The sad truth I most often witnessed was that people died as they had lived. It took a special kind of person to have the courage to admit they had got it wrong and that they needed help.

The thief on the cross had that courage, the courage to ask Jesus to remember him when he came into his kingdom. We aren't told what it was about this thief that gave him that courage. His crucified comrade in crime responded very differently, taunting Jesus to save himself and them (Luke 23:39). But reality came into sharp focus for one of the two thieves as he hung there next to Jesus. He understood that he was justly condemned for his crimes, but also that someone was hanging next to him who could help. 'Jesus, remember me when you come into your kingdom,' was his simple plea. 'Truly I tell you, today you will be with me in paradise,' came Jesus' reassuring reply. I find these some of the most hopeful words in the Bible because, if this robber can receive such a promise, then so can I.

The entry point to heaven

In the last few chapters we thought about the wonderful future of the new creation, but this still leaves a question: who will be a part of this future? Is it automatic for everyone whatever they have done or believed in this life? Will everyone be a part of the new creation whether they want to be or not? How do you enter into this glorious hope of heaven on earth? To begin to answer these questions, I want us to think more about the thief on the cross.

Have you ever wondered what it was that led Jesus to promise paradise to this thief? It certainly wasn't because the thief had done more good deeds than bad deeds in his life; the thief was being crucified because he was a violent criminal. It certainly wasn't because he had led a devout religious life; probably this thief had rarely darkened the door of a synagogue. It wasn't because the thief knew the Old Testament Scriptures from back to front; Jesus didn't give him a theological quiz while they hung there on the cross. It wasn't through understanding the mechanism of substitutionary atonement that this thief was saved,[1] even though the sacrifice that would pay the

1 Substitutionary atonement is the theological term for the way that God provides a sacrifice in our place to pay the price for our sins.

price for his sins was taking place before his very eyes. Neither did Jesus check that the thief understood the four spiritual laws of salvation before offering him paradise.[2] Rather, all the thief knew was that he was guilty of his crimes, that he was facing God's judgment and that he needed help (Luke 23:40–41). And even though he was nailed to a cross, slowly dehydrating and suffocating to death, he saw something about the man nailed next to him that gave him hope that he could help.

This thief had found the entry point to the kingdom of heaven that Jesus talked about in the Beatitudes: 'Blessed are the poor in spirit, for theirs is the kingdom of heaven' (Matthew 5:3). He had the 'poverty of spirit' to know that he could not fight or buy or threaten or blackmail or earn or bargain or invent or merit his way out of the mess he was in. He knew he could not save himself, but right beside him was someone who could help. Whenever I think of this moment I am reminded of a scene in Douglas Coupland's book, *Life After God*. Coupland's novels capture the complexities and contradictions of living our modern, dislocated, social-media-saturated, angst-ridden, fast-forward lives. Although Coupland would not describe himself as a Christian, his words encapsulate for me this moment of poverty of spirit that the thief had on that cross. He writes:

> Now, here is my secret: I tell it to you with an openness of heart I doubt I shall ever achieve again, so I pray that you are in a quiet room as you hear these words. My secret is that I need God; that I am sick and can no longer make it alone. I need God to help me to give, because I no longer seem to be capable of giving; to help me to be kind, as I no longer seem capable of kindness; to help me love, as I seem beyond being able to love.[3]

2 The four spiritual laws are a commonly used evangelistic tool that some Christians think are essential to understand before one can come to faith. They are: Law 1 – God loves you and offers a wonderful plan for your life; Law 2 – humanity is sinful and separated from God; Law 3 – Jesus Christ is God's only provision for the sin of humankind; Law 4 – we must individually receive Jesus Christ as Saviour and Lord.

3 Douglas Coupland, *Life after God* (London: Simon & Schuster, 1994), pp. 357–359.

To know we need help is the entry point to the kingdom of heaven. And the good news of the gospel is that all we need to do in our poverty is to raise empty hands and receive the joy-filled gift of new life that God offers us through Jesus Christ. Nothing else is required; there is no religious duty or good deed we must perform, no magic formula we must recite, no sacred knowledge we must be initiated into, no price we need pay. As Jesus says, 'Let anyone who is thirsty come to me and drink' (John 7:37), for, 'To the thirsty I will give water without cost from the spring of the water of life' (Revelation 21:6). This is grace: God in Jesus Christ gives us what we do not deserve and cannot earn. All we have to do is trust enough to ask Jesus for his gift of new life. This is what it means to have 'faith' or to 'believe' in Jesus. The English word 'faith' comes from the Latin word *fidere*, which means to trust. Faith is when we trust Jesus to do what we cannot do ourselves, to wipe us clean of our sins and give us the everlasting life of his Holy Spirit. As the apostle John wrote: 'to all who did receive [Jesus], to those who believed in his name, he gave the right to become children of God' (John 1:12–13). It is this trust in Jesus that the penitent thief had and that we too can have. Yet how can an event that happened nearly two thousand years ago be relevant for our lives today?

Faith, the cross and time

How can an event as simple as one man dying on a hill outside Jerusalem in (approximately) AD 33 be enough to forgive the sins of everyone who has ever lived? What about those who lived before Jesus died? How can they also be forgiven by his death if it hadn't happened yet in history? To answer this, we need to visit Flatland once again.

You will remember that the citizens of Flatland live in only two dimensions, like a flat piece of paper, but the third dimension of Spaceland surrounds them even though they cannot see it. Now imagine two people in Flatland stretching out empty hands of faith to trust God. One (Point B in Figure 5 below) is *before* the event of Jesus' death (the cross in the diagram), and one (Point A) *after* the event of Jesus' death.

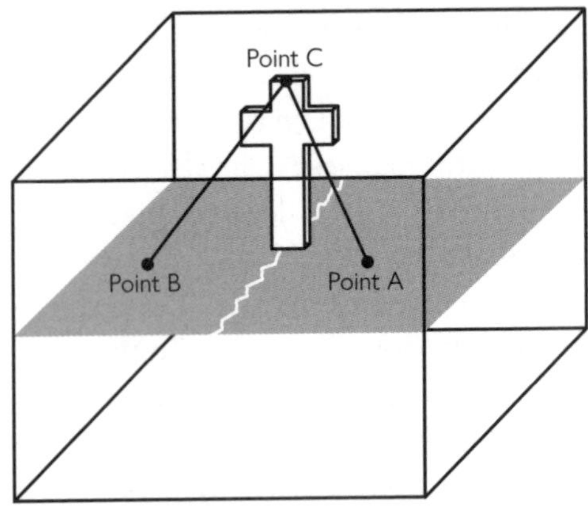

Figure 5 **Point C in Spaceland can connect points A and B, even though A and B cannot connect in Flatland**

The crucifixion, however, is not just an earthly event. In the perspective of Flatland it is just one moment in time, but Jesus is the man in whom heaven and earth meet. His death on the cross not only occurred in earthly dimensions but also took place in the eternal dimension of heaven (Point C in the diagram) because it was part of the 'eternal purpose' of God's will to save humanity (Ephesians 3:11). In a similar way, when we decide to raise empty hands of faith to God, it is an event that happens within the space–time dimensions of the earth, but it is also a heavenly event; it is in the dimension of God's will because God does not want 'anyone to perish, but everyone to come to repentance' (2 Peter 3:9). Points A and B can now connect to the event of the cross through the dimension of heaven (Point C), even though in earthly time Point B is before the cross and Point A after the cross. Trusting God for forgiveness and mercy can connect everyone to the cleansing event of Jesus' death through the heavenly dimension of eternity.

So when characters like Moses and Elijah from the Old Testament chose to follow God and to trust in his mercy, they too were cleansed by the sacrificial blood of Jesus Christ, just as I was, even though the cross hadn't yet happened in earthly time. Indeed, the sins of all those people who had faith in God's mercy but lived before the time of Jesus are cleansed by the cross and not by any other means, such as good deeds, even though they did not have the opportunity to know more than that they needed to lift empty hands to a gracious and merciful God. That is why Jesus can say, 'I am the way and the truth and the life. No one comes to the Father except through me' (John 14:6). His blood is the only means to cleanse people from the guilt of their sin and is the only way to the heavenly Father. How we receive that blood is exactly the same for Moses and Elijah as it is for you and me, with the empty hands of trust in a merciful and loving God who welcomes all who come to him in their need. The difference is that because we live after Jesus' death, we know the wonderful means by which God enabled our sins to be forgiven, the gift of his Holy Spirit, and the sure and certain hope of the resurrection.

Of course, there are many good questions we might want to ask about having faith in Jesus. What happens to unborn babies or children who die in infancy? And what about those who live in countries where choosing to follow Christ will lead to imprisonment or even death? These are important questions that Christians have thought long and hard about.[4] The most important foundation for any answer is the character of God himself. He is utterly, utterly just, knowing every circumstance, every situation, every mitigation and every opportunity we have ever had or ever will have. He will never make a mistake in his judgments. Even more than this, his offer of forgiveness is wide and deep, even extending to a criminal hanging on a cross for his crimes.

An invitation to a party

Being a part of the kingdom of heaven is a gift that Jesus offers us through his death and resurrection. In the Bible, when Jesus talked about this gift, he often compared it to being like an invitation to a party or a wedding feast.[5] It is not an invitation to dry religiosity or to pious legalism, or to a miserly dry crust of bread and water, but

4 If you want to explore more on these questions, see the 'Further reading and resources' section at the end of this book.

5 For examples, see Matthew 8:11; 22:2; 25:10; Luke 12:36. See also Revelation 19:9.

an invitation to join in a joyful banquet. It is a call to celebrate our restored relationship with our loving Creator God and the joy and hope of the new creation. It is a wide, generous invitation to anyone who will come. In fact, Jesus went out of his way to invite the most unexpected people to the kingdom of heaven, people that the self-sufficient religious elite of his day didn't approve of. Jesus invited those whose lives were a mess, not the happy, shiny people who had it all together. As Jesus said, it's not those who think they are healthy that want a doctor but those who know they are sick and in need of help (Mark 2:17). Jesus invited to God's party prostitutes (Luke 7:37) and pagans (Mark 7:24–30), untouchables (Matthew 8:1–4), adulterers (John 8:3–11), criminals (Luke 23:42–43), the enemies of Israel (Matthew 8:5–13) and collaborators with those enemies (Luke 7:34). That's how big the grace of God is. The question for all of us is, will we also accept the invitation to the party?

An invitation refused

Over the past few years I have presented material contained in this book in many different settings, but almost every time someone has asked, 'What about hell? What about those who don't want God's invitation?' Hell is an uncomfortable and unpopular subject to speak about today. Discussions are not helped by the fact that many of our popular images of hell owe more to the imagination of the medieval poet Dante[6] and the Greek myths of Tartarus,[7] than they do to any biblical text. When it comes to hell I feel the same as C. S. Lewis, who wrote, 'There is no doctrine which I would more willingly remove from Christianity . . . if it lay in my power.'[8] In our increasingly secular world it is not just the existence of hell that has come into question, but also the morality of a God

6 Dante Alighieri (*c.*1265–1321) wrote a grand poetic work, *The Divine Comedy*, a journey through heaven, hell and purgatory. His vision of hell had seven levels, each level assigned to tortures related to specific sins committed on earth. It came to have a powerful place in the religious imagination of Western Europe.

7 The deepest dungeon of the underworld (Hades), where those who had committed crimes against the gods were tortured in 'appropriate' ways.

8 C. S. Lewis, *The Problem of Pain* (London: Geoffrey Bles, 1956 [1940]), ch. 8, p. 106.

who can consign anyone, except perhaps the worst mass murderers and rapists, to eternal punishment.

Yet, as much as I would like to dispense with this most uncomfortable of doctrines, I find I cannot. For, as Lewis continues, 'Hell has the full support of Scripture and, especially, of our Lord's own words; it has always been held by Christendom, and it also has the support of reason.'[9] However much I would like to, I cannot get away from the conclusion that not everyone will participate in the party of the new creation. Some will miss out on this glorious future of heaven on earth.

In the parables where Jesus describes the kingdom of heaven as a party or a wedding banquet, he talks about those who refuse this invitation; some are preoccupied by the busyness of life (Matthew 22:5); others think they have more important things to do (Luke 14:18–20); some wilfully ignore the invitation; others even go so far as to kill the messengers (Matthew 22:6); some receive the summons but when it comes to it they don't get ready for the wedding (Matthew 25:1–13) or try to get into the banquet without wedding clothes (Matthew 22:11–13). In the end, all these people will find themselves shut out in darkness from the joyful celebration progressing within the feasting hall (Matthew 22:13; 25:11; Luke 13:25). With 'weeping and gnashing of teeth' they will want to join in the party, but they will find the doors have closed against them (Matthew 8:12; 13:42; 22:13; 24:51; 25:30; 25:46; Luke 13:28).

Regret at missing out

If I was to sum up the experience of 'weeping and gnashing of teeth', I would use the word 'regret'. Weeping is a sign of grief at what could have been; gnashing of teeth is a mixture of jealousy at what others have and sorrow for what we have missed out on. It seems that Jesus is describing the sudden realization that something wonderful, something glorious, something joyful was offered but we ignored it and refused it. We shut the doors on it. We pushed it away, saying

9 Lewis, *The Problem of Pain*, ch. 8, p. 106.

we had better things to do and would think about it another time. However, one day the time will have passed, and the opportunity will be gone, and the doors to the party will have closed, with us on the other side.

It is important to notice that in these parables Jesus focuses this warning of regret on the religious leaders of Israel. As we have seen, the people of Israel had a unique place in God's plan to bring heaven to earth, but instead of being a light that pointed the pagan nations towards heaven, the priests of Israel had become obsessed with legal and racial purity. They excluded the very people that Jesus came to earth to welcome into his kingdom (Matthew 23:13). These parables of missing out on the party are warnings to the religious people of Jesus' day that their wilful refusal to recognize what God is doing through him will lead to them being shut out from the coming kingdom while others take their places at the wedding feast (Matthew 8:11–12). It is also a warning today, not to the poor and needy but to churchgoing Christians, that a dry self-protective religiosity is not the entrance to the kingdom of heaven. If we want to be a part of heaven we must be prepared to be a part of what God is doing on earth.

The reality of justice

I find the thought that some will be excluded from the new creation an uncomfortable truth in today's tolerant world. But, like Lewis, I am compelled to accept it, not only because of Jesus' words but also because of the evidence of reason. Some years ago, I was watching a BBC documentary about the Cambodian dictator Pol Pot, whose Khmer Rouge communist party murdered more than 1 million of their own people. It was especially poignant because I was watching with a German friend who had recently been to Cambodia and visited the museum in Phnom Penh, which catalogued the crimes of Pol Pot's regime. The BBC reporter bemoaned how few of those who had organized and carried out this genocide had ever faced justice. Pol Pot himself lived in comparative luxury until his death in 1998. 'It's so terrible that he has just got away with it and will never stand trial for what he did,' lamented my friend. 'That is true if the earth is all there is,' I replied, 'but if Christianity is true, and the God of the Bible does exist, then Pol Pot will have had to answer for his crimes.'

The first reason that some must miss out on heaven is because of justice. The Bible tells us that each of us will be judged for the things we have done (or left undone) in our lives on earth (Hebrews 9:27). We tend to think of a God who will judge us as bad news. Yet it is actually good news, because it means there really is justice in this world and that people like Pol Pot will not get away with the crimes they have committed. A God who judges means that the murder of 1 million people really does matter. If the origin of our universe is merely amoral inanimate matter, then ultimately there is no-one to call us to account for what we have done with our lives; you can kill a million people and get away with it. But a God who judges, no matter how uncomfortable that might make us feel, means that justice for people like Pol Pot is a reality. But if this is true, then we must come to the uncomfortable conclusion that one day we also must give an account to God for how we have lived our lives on this earth.

What, then, is God's judgment of someone like Pol Pot? Surely it must be that Pol Pot cannot be a part of God's new creation because he is not fit to be a part of it. How can he be when his heart was indifferent to the suffering of the million people who were trampled to death by his grandiose schemes? When Jesus comes to earth again and all evil is finally destroyed, then surely Pol Pot must be destroyed too, otherwise he would reinfect the new creation with his heart of darkness. Yet, this problem is not just one that Pol Pot faces. It is a problem for every one of us. We may not have committed crimes as heinous as Pol Pot's and neither are our hearts so given over to evil. Yet we have taken part in the disintegration of God's good creation and the wounding of other people. We all have hearts that are unfit to be a part of heaven on earth. None of us is worthy to be a part of the kingdom of heaven, which is exactly why God sent Jesus from heaven to earth.

God gave his one and only Son to be the answer to the reality of justice. That is why Christ died on the cross. His blood was shed as the sacrifice that would pay for our guilt and for the guilt of all humanity – even for Pol Pot's guilt. Christ died for Pol Pot too. His crimes, immense as they are, also can be cleansed by the sacrifice of Christ on the cross. When the infinite God died, his life was enough to wipe away the sins of the whole human race. As shocking as it might seem, Pol Pot could also receive God's life-giving Spirit and become a part of the kingdom of heaven, if only he would be willing to raise his empty hands and ask for the forgiveness and new life that Christ offers. Justice is the first reason that we cannot dispense with the reality that some people will be separated from the kingdom of heaven for ever, but there is another reason too.

The necessity of freedom

It has become popular among some Christians to believe that everyone will be saved no matter what we have done in our lives, that God will forgive us all in the end and everyone will be a part of the new creation. I certainly find this an attractive idea because it makes God out to be the very epitome of tolerance, the virtue that we prize most highly in modern Western culture. However, this idea of universal salvation raises another question: the question of freedom and the dignity of human choice.

Freedom is central to the Christian world view. God did not create humans as automatic machines, but as beings who can think and choose and act. The most important decision and action we can make is to love God and to love others (Matthew 22:34–40) because we are made in the image of the God who is love (1 John 4:16). But love must be chosen in order to be love. It cannot be forced or coerced. God honours our freedom so highly that he even allows us to reject his love, as Adam and Eve did. Yet even when they did so, God did not take away their freedom. He did not force them back into relationship with himself, but instead asked them questions so that they might think about what they had done and then choose to return to him of their own free will. The same is true throughout the Bible narrative. God didn't force himself on Jacob when he was on the run in the wilderness, or on the people of Israel at Mount Sinai, and in the same way God will never force himself on us. Instead, he showed his love by sending his Son to die in our place and by giving us his Holy Spirit to change our hard hearts, so that we might choose to receive his gift of love and become his children. Being a part of the new creation is not just about living for eternity in a nice place – it is being welcomed into the loving relationship of God himself; and that is something we must choose.

To refuse this gift is not a future that God wills for us, but it is a future that he allows us to choose if we so will it. As C. S. Lewis wrote:

> There are only two kinds of people in the end: those who say to God, 'Thy will be done,' and those to whom God says, in the end, 'Thy will be done.' All that are in Hell, choose it. Without that self-choice there could be no Hell. No soul that seriously and constantly desires joy will ever miss it. Those who seek find. Those who knock it is opened.[10]

We have been invited to the wonderful party of the new creation. If at the end we find the doors to the feasting hall are closed, we will discover that it is we who have locked them from our side. [11]

Of course, there are many more questions we might want to ask about what happens to those who miss out on the new creation. To undertake a thorough discussion of the biblical, theological and ethical aspects of this topic would take an entire book, and other authors have done a far better job than I ever could.[12] Instead, in keeping with the dimensional theme of this book, I would like to focus on the question of the *dimension* of hell.

A visit to Pointland

There is an episode in the Flatland story by Edwin Abbott, where the three-dimensional Sphere journeys to Pointland, a land of only one

---

10 C. S. Lewis, *The Great Divorce* (London: Fount, 1997 [1946]), ch. 9, p. 58.

11 This idea is from Lewis, *The Problem of Pain*, ch. 8, p. 115.

12 For books that discuss the debates over the nature of hell, see Edward William Fudge and Robert A. Peterson, *Two Views of Hell: A biblical and theological dialogue* (Downers Grove, IL: IVP, 2000); Christopher W. Morgan and Robert A. Peterson (eds), *Hell Under Fire* (Grand Rapids, MI: Zondervan, 2004); or Denny Burk, John G. Stackhouse et al., *Four Views on Hell* (Grand Rapids, MI: Zondervan, 2nd edn, 2016).

dimension. There he meets a Point, a one-dimensional being. The point is 'himself his own World, his own Universe; of any other than himself he can form no conception . . . he has no cognisance even of the number Two; nor has he a thought of Plurality; for he is himself his One and All, being really nothing'.[13] The Sphere tries to tell the Point about the existence of more dimensions, but the Point, being unable to conceive of any other except himself, interprets his words as if they were his own thoughts. Nothing the Sphere can do or say can penetrate the Point's defences. There is nothing that 'can rescue him from his self-satisfaction'.[14]

If heaven is the expansion of dimensions, Pointland captures well the quality of hell; hell is the contraction of dimensions until all that exists is a single all-consuming point. If heaven is the deepening of joy-filled relationship with God, with other people and with his creation, then hell is, to use Luther's phrase, 'man turned inwards upon himself'; humanity sucked ever deeper into the black hole of selfishness until there is no longer any possibility of love for God, for others, or indeed for anyone or anything outside of the self. If heaven is the addition of depth and meaning and glory to the earth, then hell is the reduction of the earth into shallowness, insignificance and emptiness. If heaven is life in all its fullness, an eternity of enriched and thickened time, then hell is the emptying of life and the futility of time wasted. It is not surprising, then, that one of the words the Bible uses to describe this state is Hades,[15] the monochrome shadow world of the Greek underworld.

A hellish direction to life on earth

In Chapter 4 we thought about the way that sin introduced a new direction to creation. God created the earth to be expanded by the dimension of heaven, but sin redirected it towards hell, towards the diminishment of dimensions. Sin takes all the good gifts and

13 Edwin A. Abbott, *Flatland: A romance of many dimensions* (1884).

14 Abbott, *Flatland*.

15 The New Testament uses the Greek word *Hades* ten times in total. Examples are Matthew 11:23, Luke 16:23 and Revelation 20:13–14.

abilities that God gave human beings and uses them for self-serving ends. When we do so, we make the earth a more hellish place rather than a more heavenly one. When we do so, we become like trees without fruit. We don't produce good things that we can share and that give life to others. In the Gospels there are many places where Jesus warns people that trees without fruit are only fit to be cut down and thrown as waste on the burn pile.[16]

This is why Jesus wants us to take sin seriously. He's not being just moralistic. Sin really matters because it has a way of infecting our lives so that we become like barren trees, sucking all the nutrients of life into ourselves but producing no fruit that gives life to others. Jesus therefore warns his listeners that if some part of our lives leads us to sin, then it is better to throw that part on to the waste heap than let it infect the whole of our lives and risk being thrown onto the fire ourselves (Matthew 5:27–30).[17] I once talked with a young man with such a severe pornography addiction that his whole life was disintegrating around him. He had failed his university courses and was so lost in a fantasy world that he had become cut off from any real relationships. He took the decision to get rid of any internet access at home and only use a computer in public places where he could not look at porn without others seeing. That was his response to taking the effects of sin seriously in his life. He threw his internet router on to the rubbish dump rather than let it infect his whole being and make his life a meaningless waste.

The earth is a battleground between heaven and hell, and we are in the midst of that battle. Satan wants to collapse reality into himself and pull the whole earth into his all-consuming orbit. But God has sent his Son into the world to give us life, life in all its fullness. The battle is not just about individuals, but is also at the level of ideas. It is a struggle between truth and lies, because lies can send whole cultures in a hell-bound direction, as the world witnessed in Nazi Germany and Pol Pot's Cambodia. Every choice we make is a

16 Matthew 3:8–10; 7:15–19.

17 Jesus often uses the word 'Gehenna' to describe this place of fiery destruction. The name is taken from the valley of Ben Hinnom outside Jerusalem which is where the Israelites sacrificed their own children by fire in worship of false gods (see 2 Kings 23:10; Jeremiah 7:31; 32:35).

movement towards one or the other. Every time we make a choice to use other people as objects to be manipulated and consumed, we bring the earth a little closer towards hell, and we become a little less human, a little less heavenly and bit more hellish. Every time we choose to be a life-giving gift, we grow in our humanity and make the little piece of earth where we live a little more heavenly. In his essay, 'The Weight of Glory', Lewis reflects on the serious responsibility of our actions in the world and towards one another: 'All day long we are, in some degree, helping each other to one or other of these destinations . . . it is immortals whom we joke with, work with, marry, snub, and exploit – immortal horrors or everlasting splendours.'[18] However, we are not without hope in this battle.

The hope of heaven on earth

As we have seen, there is only one winner in the struggle for the planet earth. The war may not yet be over, but Jesus has won the decisive battle on the cross. His death has opened the way between dimensions, and nothing can now stop the final marriage of heaven and earth when Jesus comes again. Until then, Jesus has sent his Spirit to dwell within those of us who reach out to him with empty hands of faith, so that we can be a part of the eternal kingdom of heaven on earth. Heaven is not just about the life to come but, as we shall see in the last chapter, it is about life here and now on earth.

The story of the Bible is the story of God's grace to graceless humanity. It is the story of God bringing heaven to earth so that it might be saved from hell. Each of us, like the thief on the cross, has a choice to make: to receive God's gift or to refuse it. The feasting hall is lit and decorated; the table is set and a delicious meal prepared; the wine goblets are filled to overflowing; the invitation has been sent. But the choice is ours. Will you come to the party?

18 C. S. Lewis, 'The Weight of Glory', in *C. S. Lewis, Essay Collection: Faith, Christianity and the church* (London: HarperCollins, 2000 [1949]), pp. 105–106.

12

An earth-dweller's guide to participating in heaven on earth

> Your kingdom come,
> your will be done,
> on earth as it is in heaven.
> (Jesus, the Sermon on the Mount, Matthew 6:10)

I started this book with two questions: 'What is heaven? and 'Where is heaven?' Over the previous chapters we have seen that heaven is not a location within space, but the dimension of reality where God's will is done. We have also seen that the story of the Bible is not about us escaping into an other-worldly heaven, but about the coming of the kingdom of heaven to be right here among us on earth. The end of God's story is not the destruction of the world but its restoration in the new creation of a united heaven and earth. In the last few chapters we have thought about what it will be like in this new creation. But I want to end by thinking about the practical implications of the kingdom of heaven for our lives here and now on earth.

Karl Marx accused Christianity of being the 'opium of the masses' because he believed that its promise of a life to come prevented Christians from taking action over the stark realities of life now on earth. However, as we have seen, the gospel is not about Christians living spiritually pure lives while they wait to go to heaven; it is about the power of heaven coming to transform the earth into a heavenly place. In the Lord's Prayer, Jesus taught his disciples to pray, 'your kingdom come, your will be done, on earth as it is in heaven'. This is a prayer for heaven, the dimension of God's will, to be done on earth. It isn't in some distant future that God wants his will to be done, but now on earth, in the messiness of everyday life. Heaven is not some faraway place but a dimension that is present on earth right here and right now, wherever God's will is done by those filled with his love and empowered by his Spirit to live lives characterized by relationships of love. The gospel is an invitation to each of us to participate in the dimension of heaven and to play our unique part in the story of heaven coming to earth.

Bridgeheads of heaven on earth

As we have seen, through the gift of the Holy Spirit, Christians are touching places of heaven on earth, bridgeheads of heaven in enemy-occupied territory, doorways through which the power of heaven can flow out to the earth. A bridgehead is a military term used to describe a secure area in enemy-occupied territory, from which an invasion can begin. On D-Day, the Allies established a bridgehead on the beaches of northern France, from where the liberation of Nazi-occupied Europe could begin. If you are a Christian, then you are a bridgehead of heaven on earth, from where the liberating power of heaven can flow out to bring new life to the sin-infected earth. You and other Christians with whom you meet are mini temples where God is present on earth; places where the power of heaven is at work to restore and renew a world spoiled by sin. Christians are not just earth-dwellers but are also citizens of heaven (Philippians 3:20), citizens of heaven on earth. This heavenly citizenship does not mean Christians are waiting to escape into heaven but, rather, that they have the mission of bringing God's healing and restoring love to earth. The gospel is an invitation to each of us to play our unique part in this mission.

Being a part of bringing heaven to earth involves much more than just telling people about the good news of Jesus Christ. It means living out that good news in every aspect of our lives on earth. Of course, telling other people about the gift that Jesus offers is vital, because it is through trusting Christ that we become a part of the dimension of heaven. However, God does not just want to redeem our souls. As Paul says in his letter to the Ephesians, the mystery of

God's will is to 'bring unity to all things in heaven and on earth under Christ' (Ephesians 1:10). The mission that God gives his heavenly citizens on earth is none other than the mission he gave humanity in the garden of Eden: to rule with him in bringing the loving order of heaven to earth until the whole earth is a heavenly place. How exactly do we do that? How can we be a part of bringing heaven to earth?

Opening our eyes to the dimension of heaven on earth

In his letter to the Colossians, Paul encourages his readers to set their hearts and minds 'on things above, not on earthly things' (Colossians 3:1–4). This is not a command to think only about heaven and have as little as possible to do with everyday life on earth; it is an encouragement to expand our minds so that we can see what the everyday things of earthly life would look like if they were transformed by the dimension of heaven.

One of the problems for the religious elite of Jesus' day is that they did not have eyes that could see what the dimension of heaven looked like on earth. When Jesus healed a man born blind, the religious leaders could only see that Jesus had broken the law by healing on the Sabbath (John 9:1–41). They failed to see the healing as a sign of the restoring power of the kingdom of heaven coming to earth. The Pharisees were like Flatlanders, locked into a two-dimensional perspective, when right in front of them was the wonder of the third dimension. If we are to take part in the kingdom of heaven, we need to learn to be heavenly minded. This does not mean thinking of some far-off ethereal future, but thinking about what this square inch of the world in front of me would look like if it was transformed by the power of heaven.

In the Sermon on the Mount, Jesus gives us illustrations of what bringing heaven to earth might look like when he talks about things like 'turning the other cheek', 'going the extra mile' or 'loving our enemies'. In these examples, Jesus invites us to imagine how things could be different if we allowed the kingdom of heaven to be at work through us. To do this we must have 'renewed minds' that can see beyond the patterns of our earth-bound lives. Then we will be able to see what God's will is – 'his good, pleasing and perfect will' – for the square inch of the world in which we live (Romans 12:2).

Being heavenly minded does not mean that we construct a Disneyland view of the world where we only allow ourselves to see good things and turn a blind eye to evil. It does not mean that we escape into a Christian or church 'bubble', where we try to insulate ourselves from the 'sinful world out there'. Being heavenly minded means that we ask God to open our eyes so we can see the hurt and pain of the broken world around us. It means we ask God to open our eyes so we can see where we are at fault and a part of that hurt and pain. As Jesus pointed out, it is a sad truth that we are often blind to our own sins while all too easily pointing the finger at others (Matthew 7:3–5). Many parts of the church have taken far too long to speak out against the injustices of racism or sexism, to repent, ask forgiveness and seek reconciliation not only for past wrongs but also for current attitudes.

Being heavenly minded means more than seeing what is wrong with the world; it means seeing how we can be a part of the transforming love of God in our square inch of the world. A few months ago I was talking to a Christian man who worked for a parking enforcement agency. Probably most of us could not imagine anywhere further away from the kingdom of heaven than handing out parking tickets! This man had just been promoted to a management role and wanted to think through what it meant to bring heaven into his place of work. So he prayed and asked God to open his eyes to the kingdom of heaven in his square inch of the earth. The first conclusion he came to was to bring indoor plants into his workspace. Their office was drab and grey, and totally devoid of any beauty, not even having windows where one could see the world outside. He had decided to bring indoor plants into the space to bring something that would speak of the beauty of God's creation. He also decided that he would meet every few weeks with each of the employees he supervised and invite them to sit down and have a cup of tea or coffee with him. He would listen to them, not just about the stresses and difficulties of the work but also about their hobbies and interests, their families and relationships, and other things going on in their lives. He wanted to witness to the reality of heaven by treating his co-workers as human beings made in the image of God, not just as cogs in the parking enforcement system. These two things may seem like small things, but they were ways that God showed him of bringing something of heaven to a parking enforcement office. Seeing the earth in the perspective of heaven is not something that comes naturally to earth-dwellers. It is something we can only do with the help of the power of heaven.

Trusting in the power of heaven not in earthly power alone

As we have seen, the story of redemption is not the story of how human cleverness and ingenuity brought heaven and earth back together. Redemption is the story of how God opened doorways between dimensions so that the power of heaven could restore the sin-infected earth. If we are going to take part in the new creation, we cannot do it in our own strength or cleverness. We need help from heaven, which is why Jesus gave the gift of his Holy Spirit.

Francis and Edith Schaeffer, the founders of L'Abri Fellowship, wrote of the importance of the 'distinction between people (even consecrated people) building Christ's Church, and *Christ* building his Church through converted and consecrated people'.[1] In creation, God invited human beings to be creative builders, craftsmen and women of heaven on earth, but we were to put into practice the overall plan and design of the Great Architect of Creation. It was when humans attempted to usurp the role of God and become themselves the grand architects of reality that sin distorted the world. If we are to be a part of the coming of the kingdom of heaven to earth we cannot make this same mistake. It has been when Christians have thought that *they* are building the kingdom of heaven that the church has become most despotic, violent and

1 The Consensus of Faith/Basic Principles of Operation of L'Abri Fellowship (1955) are available at <www.labri.org/statements/The-LAbri-Statements.pdf>.

abusive. Instead, we must always remember that being a part of the kingdom of heaven means being a part of what *God* is doing on earth; it means being a part of the 'way of heaven' that Jesus taught in the Sermon on the Mount, and that he lived out not in dominating power but in his sacrificial love for us on the cross.

Just as Jesus had to do when he was tempted in the wilderness and in Gethsemane, we have to trust in God's way rather than try to take matters into our own hands, as if we know better than God. Trusting God's way means humility, prayerfulness and waiting.[2]

We must have humility because we have to admit that we are often as much a part of the problem as the solution. It is often our words and actions that damage God's good creation and hurt other people. Humility means we must recognize that it is I who need to change if I am to be a part of heaven on earth, and that if I am going to change I need the power of heaven, because I cannot change in my own strength. It is this power that Jesus sent to us in his Holy Spirit. It is as we receive his Spirit and enter ever more deeply into relationship with our heavenly Father, that we are healed and restored by his love to become more in his image. God is overflowing, other-centred love and when we are empowered by his love we too are enabled to love others, even those we may count as enemies. If we are to do this, then prayerfulness is essential to bringing the loving rule of heaven to earth.

The very act of praying is an admission that we don't have all the answers ourselves. It acknowledges that the kingdom of heaven is not about our agenda, but about God's will. To pray is to recognize that we do not know how to bring heaven to our square inch of the earth and that, even if we did, we do not have the resources to do it, nor the love to put what we see into practice. As we pray, we must also wait. We must wait to see what God is wanting to do in a certain situation rather than rush into our own plans and schemes to 'improve' the world. Our earth-bound minds are filled with notions

2 If you want to explore further what it means to trust God through humility, prayerfulness and waiting, I recommend Francis Schaeffer's book, *No Little People* (Downers Grove, IL: IVP, 1974), especially the chapters titled 'The Weakness of God's Servants' and 'The Lord's Work in the Lord's Way'.

of 'bigger is better' or 'efficiency is everything' or 'I need lots of followers to make an impact', but the economy of the kingdom of heaven is different. We need to ask God to show us and teach us and equip us, trusting that if we pray and wait he will answer us. As Jesus promised, 'Ask and it will be given to you; seek and you will find; knock and the door will be opened to you' (Matthew 7:7).

Some years ago at L'Abri we welcomed a group of church leaders from Eastern Europe. Most of them had been influenced by church-growth models borrowed from the business world. At breakfast one of them asked me, 'What is your five-year growth plan for L'Abri?' It was early morning, so it took me some time to process his question. We didn't have a 'growth plan' in the terms he was thinking of, but I realized we did have a plan for growth of a different kind, a kind that I think is more in line with the kingdom of heaven. 'We don't have a five-year model', I replied, 'but we do have a plan. Our plan is that each person who comes to stay with us grows so that they become more the person God created them to be. Our plan is that we should moment by moment prayerfully ask the Lord to show us how we can participate in his plan for their growth.'

Jesus compared the kingdom of heaven to yeast that is mixed into a batch of dough to make bread (Matthew 13:33). The baker does not make the bread rise, but she does have to mix the yeast into the dough. In the same way, it is not we who build heaven on earth, but we must remember to pray and wait, and then be obedient to what God shows us, if we are to be a part of the coming kingdom of heaven on earth.

Heaven is in the ordinary things of the earth

As earth-dwellers, we often think that the kingdom of heaven must be found only in unusual 'supernatural' experiences like visions, speaking in tongues or miracles. Yet if the kingdom of heaven is coming to earth, then Christianity is not about some other-worldly super-spirituality, but about seeing the ordinary, everyday things of this earth transformed by the power of heaven. For if heaven is the dimension where God's will is done, then even the ordinary everyday things of our earthly lives can be suffused with the glory of heaven when they are done within the will of God.

One of my favourite passages in *The Great Divorce* is when Lewis sees a procession moving through the foothills of heaven. There are bright spirits dancing and scattering flowers, and musicians playing instruments amid boys and girls singing. All this is being done in honour of a woman, behind whom follow cats and dogs, birds and horses. Lewis deduces that this woman must be the Virgin Mary to be so honoured, but his guide informs him that 'Her name on earth was Sarah Smith and she lived at Golder's Green'.[3] When Lewis comments that she must have been a person of particular importance, his guide replies, 'Aye. She is one of the great ones. Ye have heard that fame in this country and fame on Earth are two quite different things.'[4]

On earth, Sarah Smith may have appeared to be a nobody from nowhere special, but in the perspective of heaven she is 'one of the great ones'. This, we learn, is not because she did extraordinary things on earth, but because she was a woman who loved all things well. The abundance of life she had 'in Christ from the Father'[5] flowed over to all the people and things in her square inch of the world. Although single, her home was a place of warm hospitality: every child she met she treated as if they were her son or daughter; every beast and bird she encountered had a place in her love. She had brought the transforming power of heaven to earth, in ordinary everyday ways, so that everything she loved became its truer self. She was part of God's story of redemption in her square inch of suburbia.

Like Sarah Smith, we are ordinary people, living ordinary lives in ordinary places, but our lives can be extraordinary in the sight of heaven as we participate in bringing the kingdom of heaven to our square inch of the earth. Being a part of the kingdom of heaven is not always about changing the whole world. Some people, like

3 C. S. Lewis, *The Great Divorce* (London: Fount Paperbacks, 1997 [Geoffrey Bles, 1946]), p. 90.

4 Lewis, *The Great Divorce*, p. 90.

5 Lewis, *The Great Divorce*, p. 91.

William Wilberforce, have the God-given opportunity to bring large-scale changes to a whole society, as he did when he brought about the abolition of slavery in the British Empire, but most of us are not in such a situation. We can, however, bring the kingdom of heaven to our square inch of the world by loving well the people and the things of the earth where we live; for to love well is to obey the will of God, and heaven is where the will of God is done. As we love well, we can be a part of the kingdom of heaven on earth in small yet profound ways. We are uniquely placed to bring the life of heaven to our square-inch of the earth, because we know that square inch better than anyone else.

We find this emphasis on the everydayness of spirituality in the letters of the New Testament, where the apostles write about how the gospel has an impact on everyday aspects of our earthly lives. They talk about relationships between husbands and wives, parents and children, slaves and masters (Ephesians 5:21 – 6:9); about the way we use words and speak to one another (James 3:1–12); about sex (1 Corinthians 6:12–20); about our attitude to money (1 Timothy 6:6–10); and about those in authority (Romans 13:1–7). They do not just write about extraordinary supernatural things, but they talk about how the kingdom of heaven can be present in the ordinary things of everyday life.

If we think back to Genesis, we see this was how God created the world. In the garden of Eden there was no separation between sacred things and ordinary things. Heaven was combined with the ordinary everyday things of the earth because everything in Eden was in the dimension of God's will. In the new creation, God is bringing heaven and earth together again, so that the ordinary things of this life are once more the sacred things of heaven. The kingdom of heaven is present in the simplest of acts; it is present when we offer a cup of tea and an arm around a shoulder to comfort someone who is hurting; it is present in the thoughtfulness necessary to carry out practical acts of kindness and care; it is present in gentleness and generosity; in going the extra mile; in the humility to ask for forgiveness; in the patience to listen; in the faithfulness to keep promises; in the courage to tell the truth; in praying for those who hate us; in welcoming those who are different; in using our creativity to make things beautiful; in caring for God's world and his creatures. Being a part of the kingdom of heaven is about bringing the loving order of heaven into all the ordinary things of everyday life. It is also about bringing heaven into *every* area of human life.

Bringing heaven to every aspect of earthly life

Some people expect the kingdom of heaven to be concerned only with 'spiritual' things, like reading the Bible or praying, church worship, evangelism, prophecies and visions. However, as we have seen, it is God's will to 'bring unity to all things in heaven and on earth under Christ' (Ephesians 1:10). The kingdom of heaven is coming to earth not just to redeem 'church things' or 'theological things' or 'religious things' or 'supernatural things', but 'all things'. God's will is that the kingdom of heaven should bring every area of life on earth under Christ.

As we saw in Chapter 3, God intended human civilization to be a display of his marvellous wisdom in creation. All the different aspects of human culture – family, community, parenting, education, science, technology, the arts, ecology, engineering, psychology, sociology, politics, government, law, architecture – all these areas of human life were given by God to be ways in which human beings could bring the loving order of heaven to the earth. Sin distorted all of these as they became directed to self-serving ends, but the 'yeast' of the kingdom of heaven is coming to redeem them all so that they can once more be a part of heaven on earth. And every Christian has a unique part to play.

In the same passage where Paul urges Christians to 'be transformed by the renewing of your mind', he goes on to say that although Christians are one body, each has different gifts that they can use in the kingdom of heaven. Some have the wisdom to apply God's word to current cultural situations,[6] some have the gift of

6 I take this as the meaning of the gift of prophecy.

serving, some teaching, some the gift of encouraging, others giving, some leading, some showing mercy (Romans 12:4–18). Paul's point is that we are each to use the gifts, opportunities and passions that we have been given, to bring heaven to every area of earthly life in which we are involved. God's will is that all of life should be brought under the lordship of Jesus Christ. We cannot save the whole world – we are finite beings with limited time and energy – but we can, with the help of the Holy Spirit, be a part of saving our square inch of the world.[7] The question that each of us should prayerfully ask is, 'What does it look like for the area of life I am involved in to be redeemed by the dimension of heaven?' Since working at L'Abri I have had the privilege of meeting Christians in almost every walk of life who are attempting to allow the kingdom of heaven to redeem and restore those areas so that they are a blessing to the earth. I have met a Christian architect who seeks to design spaces that encourage people to relate to one another rather than live in isolation; a Christian farmer who works alongside people with mental disabilities on his land, and farms in a way that preserves the biodiversity of God's creation; a Christian mother who has started poetry-writing groups where people from different racial backgrounds can begin to understand one another; a Christian economist who tries to implement policies that focus on people not just money. All of these are attempting to bring the kingdom of heaven to the square inch of life they love and care about. This task, however, is not an easy one.

Being part of heaven on earth is a struggle

Although Jesus' death opened the way for the power of heaven to come to earth, heaven is not yet fully here. God has established a bridgehead of heaven on earth in every person who has received the

7 I first heard the idea of 'saving our square inch' at a talk given by the author Charles Strohmer, but I think it originally comes from the Dutch Christian philosopher Abraham Kuyper, who said, 'There is not a square inch in the whole domain of our human existence over which Christ, who is Sovereign over all, does not cry: "Mine!"' From a lecture on 'Sphere Sovereignty', given at the Free University, Amsterdam, 1880.

gift of his Spirit, but the earth is still a battleground between good and evil. The renewing power of heaven is here, but there are still forces of chaos at work that would frustrate and derail God's loving plan for his creation. This is not just true outside the Christian church, but also in the church and in the lives of Christians, because Christians also battle with the wounds of the past and the temptations of the present.

So Christians should not be triumphalist about the kingdom of heaven and think that things on earth will just get better and better until everything is perfect. We should take seriously Jesus' parable of the wheat and the weeds (Matthew 13:24–39) and be ready for the struggle that it is to participate in the kingdom of heaven. This struggle is not just against flesh and blood but also against more fundamental forces of evil that are working to throw off the rule of heaven (Ephesians 6:12). This is why in the Lord's Prayer Jesus teaches his disciples to pray for protection from temptation and from evil. Yet we can trust Jesus that even though the way of heaven may be hard work now, one day a harvest will come when wheat and weeds are separated once and for all. Until that day, we are engaged in a struggle that affects all areas of life – our work, our communities, our churches, our families and relationships, marriages, government and politics, our schools and universities, our creativity, the science we do and the technologies we develop. Not one single area of life is untouched by this battle.

Some Christians are always looking for a magic solution to this struggle. They are constantly searching for the latest prayer technique or spiritual programme that will make the kingdom of heaven a success on earth. When this latest thing fails, they are often filled with disappointment that eventually turns to disillusionment and cynicism. Yet there is no other way to be a part of heaven on earth than the way of humility, prayer and waiting. We must ask God to show us how to be a part of heaven on earth and to enable us, by his Spirit, to be obedient to what he shows us to do. If the kingdom of God is to advance on earth then it can only be through the readiness to admit our own failures, through the willingness to offer and receive forgiveness, and through dependence on the work of God among us. Yet even though our attempts may be imperfect and faltering, they never go to waste.

Our hope of heaven on earth is not in vain

Many people today struggle with questions about the significance of their lives: is there any meaning to these few short years we get to spend on earth? This is a valid question if we believe that the universe is merely the product of the blind forces of time and chance. I have also met Christians who struggle with meaning, who believe that nothing they do on earth has any lasting significance because when Jesus comes again he will destroy the earth and everything in it. Yet deep down all of us long for our lives to have meaning. We want the things we do and the relationships we have to be affirmed as worthwhile. Just as a small child cries out, 'Daddy, Daddy, look at me, look at what I am doing', we too need someone to see and value the things we do.

In the Gospels, Jesus encourages us that our heavenly Father does indeed see our lives. However, he does not value us in the same way that social media does. He sees beyond the exciting veneer of photo-shopped moments. God sees the small everyday acts of love that no-one else notices, the things that we do when no-one is looking but that are nonetheless part of the kingdom of heaven (Matthew 6:6). God values the things that the world says are a waste of time and energy. In the new creation the acts of love we have done in this life will 'shine like the dawn' (Psalm 37:6) as part of the glory of the kingdom of heaven on earth. Jesus says we are like a servant who has been put in charge while his master is away. When the master returns, the trustworthy servant will be greeted with the words, 'Well done, good and faithful servant! You have been faithful with a few things; I will put you in charge of many things. Come and share your master's happiness!' (Matthew 25:21).

Although participating in the kingdom of heaven on earth is now a struggle, that struggle is not without hope. Christ's death on the cross has defeated sin and death and nothing can stop the marriage of heaven and earth. We can then 'stand firm' in our faith and give ourselves 'fully to the work of the Lord', because our 'labour in the Lord is not in vain' (1 Corinthians 15:58). Everything we do on earth that is part of God's will is eternal because it is part of the everlasting dimension of heaven. There is a continuity between our lives now on earth and the fullness of the new creation to come. Everything we do now on earth that is a part of the kingdom of heaven will be a part of that final reality. I truly believe that even if these things are 'undone' on earth by the forces of evil, they will still not be in vain, but when Jesus comes again their glory will be revealed; they will exist for ever because they have been a part of the eternal dimension of heaven. Even though so many of the things we do in this life are a mix of good and bad, in the life to come all things will be redeemed and purified to reveal the wisdom of God in his creation. Everything we do that is a part of his will, every act of kindness, every sacrifice, every encouraging word, every time we have listened well, every time we have been a peacemaker, every time we have shown mercy, every true discovery, every progress in understanding and knowledge, every helpful invention, every work of art or design that reflects reality, every act of care for his creation, will be a part of eternity because it already is a part of his new creation.

Many years ago, on a flight to Warsaw, I discovered that I did not want to go to heaven. I could see no joy in being a disembodied soul living for eternity in an ethereal cloudscape. So I prayed, 'Lord, help me to want to go to heaven. Help me to long for heaven.' This book is the answer to that prayer. It has taken me many years to be able to see what the Scriptures say, and there is still much more to understand and much more that I will never know until heaven is fully here. But I do know that heaven is nearer than we think; heaven is not just in the future, but is already right here all around us, wherever God's will is done, and we can all be a part of bringing heaven to earth, right here and right now. Even the small things we do will be a part of the ever-increasing joy we will share with God, with one another and with all creation for eternity. Now I long to know the love of God face to face and for the fullness of his kingdom of heaven on earth. I hope that what I have set out in this book makes you excited about the future too, and that it also gives you hope for the present.

I hope to see you in heaven – here on earth.

Further reading and resources

Here are suggestions for further reading and resources on some of the issues discussed in this book.

For audio resources on a wide range of topics, including answers to objections and questions about Christian faith, I recommend the L'Abri Ideas Library (<www.labriideaslibrary.org>) and the University and Colleges Christian Fellowship audio lecture site (<www.bethinking.org>).

The Bible Project has short, animated videos that introduce you to a whole range of Bible topics, Bible overviews and biblical theology (<https://bibleproject.com>).

For a good (and fairly short) introduction to a Christian world view, I recommend Al Wolters, *Creation Regained* (Grand Rapids, MI: Eerdmans, 2nd edn., 2005), and for a very interesting comparison of the Christian trinitarian world view to monism and dualism, see Ellis Potter, *3 Theories of Everything* (Destinee Media, 2012). Ravi Zacharias, *Jesus Among Other Gods* (Nashville, TN: Thomas Nelson, 2010), is excellent in dealing with questions raised by other faiths.

If you want to read more about L'Abri, a good place to start is Edith Schaeffer, *L'Abri* (Worthing: Norfolk Press, 1969). For the cultural apologetic ideas of Francis Schaeffer, I recommend *Trilogy* (*The God Who Is There; Escape from Reason; He Is There and He Is not Silent)* (Westchester, IL: Crossway Books, 1990), and for his ideas on spirituality, Francis Schaeffer, *True Spirituality* (Wheaton, IL: Tyndale House Publishers, 1971).

For more in-depth reading on the biblical view of heaven, I heartily recommend Tom Wright's excellent *Surprised by Hope* (London: SPCK, 2007) and, at an advanced level, J. Richard Middleton, *A New*

Heaven and a New Earth: Reclaiming biblical eschatology (Grand Rapids, MI: Baker Academic, 2014).

For imaginative explorations of heaven, go no further than C. S. Lewis, *The Great Divorce* (London: Geoffrey Bles, 1946) and *The Last Battle* (London: The Bodley Head, 1956).

To read more on answers to common objections to Christian faith, Timothy Keller, *The Reason for God: Belief in an age of scepticism* (London: Hodder & Stoughton, 2009), and *Making Sense of God: An invitation to the sceptical* (London: Hodder & Stoughton, 2018) are very accessible and engaging, as is Michael Ots, *But Is It True?: Honest responses to 10 popular objections to the Christian faith* (London: IVP, 2016). C. S. Lewis, *Mere Christianity* (London: Geoffrey Bles, 1952) and *Miracles* (London: Fontana, 1960) are classic arguments for the veracity of Christian belief. For questions about the Bible, see Amy Orr-Ewing, *Why Trust the Bible?* (London: IVP, 2020), and Craig L. Blomberg, *Can We Still Believe the Bible?: An evangelical engagement with contemporary questions* (Grand Rapids, MI: Brazos Press, 2014). David Gooding and John Lennox have an excellent series, *The Quest for Reality and Significance* (6 vols.) (Belfast: Myrtlefield House, 2018–19), in which they give winsome responses to a range of important questions, from suffering and how we can know what is true to how we know what is right.

To explore the evidence for the resurrection of Jesus Christ, see Gary Habermas and Michael Licona, *The Case for the Resurrection of Jesus* (Grand Rapids, MI: Kregel Publications, 2004).

To go further into questions of science, faith and the new atheists, see John Lennox, *Gunning for God: Why the new atheists are missing the target* (Oxford: Lion, 2011), and *God's Undertaker: Has science buried God?* (Oxford: Lion, 2009). Alister McGrath also has written extensively on these topics and his latest book is well worth a read, *A Theory of Everything (that Matters): A short guide to Einstein, relativity and the future of faith* (London: Hodder & Stoughton, 2019).

To delve more deeply into the biblical creation account and its implications for the Christian world view, I recommend Christopher Watkins, *Thinking through Creation: Genesis 1 and 2 as tools of cultural critique* (Phillipsburg, NJ: P&R Publishing, 2017), plus, at an academic level, Henri Blocher, *In the Beginning: The opening chapters of Genesis* (Leicester: IVP, 1984).

Copyright acknowledgments